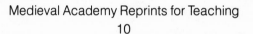
Medieval Academy Reprints for Teaching
10

Medieval Academy Reprints for Teaching

B. L. ULLMAN
INTRODUCTION BY JULIAN BROWN

Ancient Writing and its Influence

Published by University of Toronto Press
Toronto Buffalo London
in association with the Medieval Academy of America

INTRODUCTION

Berthold Louis Ullman (1882–1965) was born in Chicago and graduated from the University of Chicago in 1903. In 1908, after postgraduate work in Munich and Rome, he received his Ph.D. from Chicago for a dissertation on the text of Catullus and with it an appointment as instructor in Classics. He was head of the Department of Latin at the University of Pittsburgh (1909) and of the Department of Classics at the State University of Iowa (1919), professor of Latin at Chicago (1925), and head of the Department of Classics at the University of North Carolina (1944). Always a great traveler to the libraries of Europe, he died, still full of energy and the spirit of inquiry, while in Rome working on manuscripts in the Vatican.

As a scholar Ullman was distinguished in three fields: the transmission of classical Latin texts, including their appearances in medieval anthologies; Italian Humanism, particularly the writings and library of Coluccio Salutati; and Latin paleography, where his mastery of the other two fields allowed him to identify, in a way that is likely to stand the test of time, the originators of the two humanistic scripts. He began his work on paleography in 1906, in the Munich seminar of Ludwig Traube (1865–1907), the scholar by whose brilliant teaching and writings all subsequent work in paleography, as well as in classical and medieval Latin, has been consciously or unconsciously inspired. As an educator, in the general field and in classics, Ullman was no less active; his Latin textbooks, written with N. E. Henry and others, are widely used in the United States.[1]

Ancient Writing and Its Influence was first published in 1932. At the end of his life Ullman knew, better than anyone, that it needed revision; but he had endowed it with his own vitality, and it is the only book in English to cover, with brevity and distinction, the history of the alphabet, Greek paleography and epigraphy, Latin paleography and epigraphy, and the origins of printing.[2] Since it is still a sound intro-

---

[1] For further information on Ullman's life and publications, see especially C. Henderson, Jr. (ed.), *Classical, Mediaeval and Renaissance Studies in Honor of B. L. Ullman* (2 vols.; Rome, 1964).

[2] C. Higounet, *L'Écriture* (Collection "Que sais-je?", Paris, 1955) is comparable in scope and quality.

duction to those four closely related subjects, its right to life as a paperback is unquestionable. Meant as a short book for classicists, one of the series called "Our Debt to Greece and Rome," it says next to nothing about the scripts of the documents and records that are of prime concern to post-classical historians, and very little about the book scripts in which the Latin and vernacular literatures of the late Middle Ages were transmitted. But that omission was deliberate, and for another hand to tinker with the very individual creation of so accurate a scholar and so gifted a teacher as Ullman would be a worse impiety than to let his book be forgotten. Its new publishers have rightly decided to add only this Introduction, on the author and on the progress of research since 1932, and a Bibliographical Supplement.

If Ullman had revised *Ancient Writing,* he might have dropped from the Bibliography a few superseded or out-of-print titles; but nothing that he put in is pernicious, even now. He left out some basic works that any good university library ought to have, but he did include Thompson's *Introduction,* 1912, with its systematic bibliography of Greek and Latin paleography; and several books in the Supplement

[vii]

have bibliographies that precede 1932. Fresh
bibliographical news on all aspects of Greek,
Latin, and vernacular manuscripts may be
found in *Scriptorium*, the excellent *International
Review of Manuscript Studies* published in
Brussels (I, 1946–1947; II–XXI, 1948–
1967——). A handful of Ullman's omissions
are too puzzling to pass over. W. Wattenbach,
Das Schriftwesen im Mittelalter (3rd ed., Leipzig, 1896; reprinted Graz, 1958), is an invalu-
able compilation on books, their makers, and
the book trade. And he certainly ought to have
pointed out some of the great collections of facsimiles of pages from selected manuscripts and
some of the many complete facsimiles of manuscripts that together make the foundations of
modern paleography. The leading collections
are *Palaeographical Society* (2 series, London,
1873–1894), and *New Palaeographical Society* (2 series, London, 1903–1930); *Archivio
Paleografico Italiano* (Rome, 1882——); E.
Chatelain, *Paléographie des Classiques latins*
(Paris, 1884–1900); *Monumenta Palaeograph-
ica* (3 series, Munich, later Leipzig, 1902–
1937). The two most relevant series of complete facsimiles are *Codices graeci et latini
photographice depicti* (Leyden, 1897——) and

[viii]

Codices e Vaticanis selecti phototypice expressi (Vatican City, 1902————).

The Supplement, like Ullman's own Bibliography, is highly selective. In three of the four subjects the compiler has simply listed some handbooks, from which the reader will be able to learn more about recent publications, and added a few other titles of exceptional interest. In Latin paleography, however, because more has been written about it since 1932 than about all the other three subjects put together, and because it will doubtless be the main interest of most new readers of *Ancient Writing*, he has tried to do more. Besides handbooks and publications of basic importance, he has listed a few articles that seem particularly instructive. Work on documents and vernacular manuscripts has been omitted unless it seemed relevant to Ullman's original design.

For new work on the alphabet, see the handbooks by Cohen 1953, Higounet 1955, and Diringer 1962. The great events here have been Michael Ventris's decipherment of Linear B (Ventris and Chadwick 1956 is the basic work; Chadwick 1958 is a lucid summary), and the discovery of the Dead Sea Scrolls (Driver 1954 and 1965; Yadin 1957, and de Vaux 1961 are

[ix]

singled out because the authors are archaeologically minded). Jeffery 1961 is fundamental for writing and inscriptions in archaic Greece;[3] Woodhead 1959 is a good general handbook of Greek epigraphy.

In Greek paleography there are handbooks by van Groningen 1955 and Wittek 1967 (the latter well illustrated); Devréesse 1954 is a guide to all aspects of Greek manuscripts, including their contents. The publication of Greek papyri continues unabated (Turner 1968 is an indispensable introduction to all the problems involved; Roberts 1956 is a basic for the literary scripts, Seider 1967 for the documentary). The interactions of the Greek and Latin scripts under the Roman Empire is attracting attention (e.g., Masai 1956). The paleography of the Byzantine period has far to go, but Irigoin 1958 augurs well for the application of methods developed in the Latin field.

In Latin paleography, the great general series like the *Palaeographical Society* have mostly

[3] For learned argument on the date of the arrival of the alphabet in Greece, see also papers in the *American Journal of Archaeology* by R. Carpenter (XXXVII, 1933, pp. 8–29; XLII, 1938, pp. 58–69); by Ullman himself (XXXVIII, 1934, pp. 359–381); and by R. M. Cook and A. G. Woodhead (LXIII, 1959, pp. 175–178).

ceased, their essential work done. Illustrated
paleographical catalogues of limited groups of
manuscripts have taken their place in the front
rank: Lowe's *C.L.A.* 1934—— for literary
manuscripts before A.D. 800; Bruckner and
Marichal's *Ch.L.A.* 1954—— for documents of
the same period; Bruckner 1935—— for Swiss
scriptoria; Samaran and Marichal 1959——
and Lieftinck 1964—— for dated manuscripts
in France and Holland. Bischoff's catalogue of
over 6,000 ninth-century manuscripts is ea-
gerly awaited. Two relevant series of complete
facsimiles are *Umbrae Codicum Occidentalium*
1960—— (inexpensive, varied, well edited)
and *Early English Manuscripts in Facsimile*
1951—— (with Ker 1957, indispensable for
Anglo-Saxon manuscripts). Perat, Bischoff, and
Post 1955 and Brown 1959–1963 summarize
recent developments. The best recent handbooks are Battelli 1949, Cencetti 1954, Bischoff 1957, and Foerster 1963 (alas, none is
fully illustrated). *Scriptorium* in Brussels and
the Institut de Recherche et d'Histoire des Tex-
tes at the CNRS in Paris have sponsored major
publications and fostered a wealth of new ideas.
Since the Second World War "codicology" has
entered the field at the side of paleography in

the strict, but not universal, sense of the study of scripts only; in Dain 1964 "codicology" means systematic inventorization of the texts in manuscripts; in Masai 1950 it means archaeological investigation of how books were put together, decorated, and bound (Delaissé 1956 and 1959 are the best examples of "codicological" practice). See also Kenyon 1951, Schubart 1962, Roberts 1954 (fundamental), Lesne 1938, and Bühler 1960.

For the period until the invention of Caroline minuscule in the late eighth century, *C.L.A.* and *Ch.L.A.* are now the foundations. Mallon, Marichal, and Perrat 1939 inaugurated a fruitful era in the study of Latin script before the fifth century; however, the conclusions of Mallon 1952 are not universally accepted (e.g., in Petrucci 1962). Tjäder 1954—— on the Ravenna papyri is relevant here. As specimens of Lowe's work outside *C.L.A.* one book, 1960, and one especially informative article, 1958, must suffice. The goal of paleography in the "Caroline" period, ninth to twelfth centuries, is to ascribe manuscripts to the scriptoria of particular religious houses or churches. Exemplary publications here are Bischoff and Hoffman 1952 and Bischoff 1960 for the earlier part,

Mynors 1939 and Ker 1960 for the later. The collected papers of Traube's two successors at Munich, Lehmann 1941–1962 and Bischoff 1966–1967, illustrate both the techniques of paleography and its power to advance the history of culture.

In the "Gothic" period, thirteenth to sixteenth centuries, the problem is to impose some order on the bewildering multitude of manuscripts produced by the now mainly secular book trade. Samaran and Marichal 1959—— and Lieftinck 1964—— are especially valuable. Kruitwagen 1942 and Bischoff, Lieftinck, and Battelli 1954 deal with what to call the scripts (Lieftinck 1964—— contains important second thoughts). Destrez 1935 and Delaissé 1959 are vital for the trades in university textbooks and in "manuscrits de luxe," respectively.

Study of the humanistic scripts is the newest branch of Latin paleography, and *Ancient Writing* was the first handbook to give it a separate chapter. For the pre-humanist modifications of Italian Gothic script, Ullman 1963 and Petrucci 1967 are basic. Ullman 1960 deals with the invention of both the round hand, by Poggio Bracciolini, and the cursive, by Niccoló Niccoli. Over fifty years after his attendance of Traube's seminar, this work set him in the first rank of Latin paleographers. Wardrop 1963 is equally important for the period 1450–1550, and Casamassima 1966 for the sixteenth century. Fairbank and Hunt 1960 is perfect as a short introduction to humanistic script in Italy and England before about 1600. *Italia Medioevale e Umanistica* (Padua 1958———), contains many good articles, some by Ullman himself. Since 1962 Fairbank has contributed important notes to the *Journal of the Society for Italic Handwriting* (London). For modern times, see Morison 1951 and Fairbank 1960: paleography does *not* end with the Middle Ages.

To early type design, Morison 1962 (admirable) and Johnson 1966 are useful introductions. Febvre and Martin 1958 (ambitious) and Steinberg 1961 (modest and most business-like) cover the history of printing as a whole. Scholderer 1963 is a gem by a master. Bühler 1960 is unique, since the author has the learning to treat fifteenth-century book production as a whole, ignoring the customary barrier between work on manuscripts and work on printed books. Stevenson 1961 is essential for the proper understanding of watermarks in paper.

Ancient Writing, since it is so short, had to

[xiv]

ignore the subjects of illumination and decoration, bookbinding, musical notation, and the history of collections: all are inseparable members of the complex of subdisciplines involved in the study of manuscripts and early printed books. It may be worth pointing out that Delaissé 1959 is also a major work on illumination (see also Mynors 1939); that de Marinis 1952–1957 is important both for illumination and for bookbinding; and that at least a dozen titles in the Supplement are also key works in the history of collections. Ullman 1963, on Salutati's library, is a case in point; and his last major work, now being completed by Mr. Philip A. Stadter, is on the library of the Convent of San Marco in Florence.

JULIAN BROWN

Department of Paleography
King's College
University of London

CONTENTS

[xvii]

NOTE

The author desires to express his thanks to his colleague, Professor Charles H. Beeson, for reading the manuscript of this book.

Plates I to XVI illustrating inscriptions and manuscripts will be found following page 224 of the text.

ANCIENT WRITING
AND ITS INFLUENCE

ANCIENT WRITING
AND ITS INFLUENCE

I. THE ORIGIN OF WRITING

AS WE look back over the history of civilization, we see the prime importance of certain inventions for man's progress. The invention, or rather, the evolution of speech was one of these epoch-making events since it made possible the coöperation of great numbers of people in social groups. It was thus not only a product of man's social instinct, but also an important factor in developing that instinct. But speech itself did not satisfy primitive man, for it was not easy to surmount the barriers of time and space by speech alone. A messenger carrying a verbal message might or might not repeat it with absolute fidelity. Tradition was a meager source of information about the past. The "invention" of writing, while not so epochal an event as that of speech, was far more important than one would at first suspect.

[3]

In Thomas Astle's succinct phrasing: [1] " The noblest acquisition of mankind is SPEECH, and the most useful art is WRITING. The first eminently distinguishes MAN from the brute creation; the second, from uncivilized savages." Breasted puts it more strongly: [2] " The invention of writing and of a convenient system of records on paper has had a greater influence in uplifting the human race than any other intellectual achievement in the career of man. It was more important than all the battles ever fought and all the constitutions ever devised."

Nor was the importance of writing ended with its first development. It is still constantly producing new and important results as one or another phase is evolved. Two of the three R's — reading and writing — are dependent upon it; the third, arithmetic, makes large use of it. The invention of printing, a thing so recent that we can appreciate the enormous changes in civilization which it has wrought, is but a stage in the history of script. The system of writing which we have inherited from the Romans has had an influence in shaping our civilization which it is impossible to measure. It is not without significance that the nations which use the Roman system of writing

[4]

are the most advanced in the world. In no field is our debt to Rome greater than in that of writing. In other fields, such as language, literature, law, architecture, there are important forms which are not derived from the Roman, but the Roman script is admittedly the best in existence, and it is only a matter of time, apparently, until it will be almost universally adopted.

Whatever the precise origin of language, it cannot be denied that an important, if not the chief, factor in its creation was the imitation of sounds. In much the same way writing grew out of the imitation or sketching of objects. The earliest form of writing was pictographic, in which the writer conveyed his ideas by means of pictures of objects. This form of crude writing was therefore an outgrowth of the art of drawing and painting. Or one may perhaps say that painting itself owes its origin in part to the desire to convey information to others. Probably there was some such motive in some of the palaeolithic paintings and carvings found in the caves of France and Spain. Pictographic writing going back to the neolithic and bronze ages has been found in many parts of Europe. A familiar example that has survived to our own times is that of the American Indians. In the nature of things, such writing is often merely an aid to memory. For example, on a Dakota buffalo robe a figure of a man covered with spots represents a winter in which smallpox was epidemic. But ideas can be more explicitly expressed. In Southern Alaska, Indian hunters who found no game drew upon a piece of wood a human figure with arms stretched out sideways to represent the idea of " nothing," another human figure with the right hand raised to the mouth to represent " eat," and a hut. The total means, therefore, " nothing to eat in the house." Such pieces of wood were put along trails and were pointed to show possible rescuers the proper direction to take.

One remarkable fact about picture writing is its general similarity in all parts of the world. The sign for " nothing " just mentioned appears in a similar form in the pictographs of the Mayas of Yucatan and in the hieroglyphics of the ancient Egyptians. The modern mother with the newest ideas of child-training will be discouraged to learn that the symbol for " child " is apparently the same in ancient Egypt, China, and North America — an infant sucking its thumb. It is obvious that in picture writing there is much imitation of gesture — a form of communicating ideas very common among primitive peoples. Even abstract ideas can be expressed by picture writing as, for example, the pipe is used as the symbol of peace.

We, too, still have traces of picture writing, such as the pointing arrow and the pointing hand used on signs and in books. Many trademarks are of this nature. The Boy Scouts also use signs of this sort for trail marks.

In the course of time, pictographs tend to become conventionalized in forms often difficult to recognize. It is in such conventionalized forms that Chinese is written. Like the Indian languages, Chinese expresses abstract ideas by concrete objects. The word for " friendship," for example, is represented by a conventionalized form of two hands, one above the other. In a similar way, we represent friendship by clasped hands. The Chinese also combine words to make new ones: so in early Chinese the word for " wife " is represented by the signs for "woman" and "broom." The greatest advance made by the Chinese was in applying a sign which had been adopted for a certain word to other words of the same sound — and there are many such words (homonyms) in Chinese.

[7]

This was a first step towards alphabetic writing. But Chinese writing has remained so complicated that one must learn at least 1500 signs and a large number of combinations of these signs.

The impossibility of conveying more than a few simple ideas by Indian pictographs and the enormous difficulty of learning to write and read Chinese are significant indications of the value of our alphabetic method of writing.

The Japanese adopted some of the Chinese characters at an early period but, because their language is polysyllabic instead of monosyllabic, as Chinese is, they were able to make a great step in advance: many of the characters represent, not words, but syllables. But the exceedingly large number of homonyms in Japanese (*kō* has fifty-five different meanings) makes it necessary for Japanese to retain many of the Chinese word signs. The Japanese schoolboy must still learn hundreds of these.

The cuneiform ("wedge-shaped") script of Babylonia had much the same history as the Chinese, but it went farther. The characteristic appearance to which it owes its name is due to the material on which it was used. The characters were inscribed with a stylus on soft clay tablets; at the point where the stylus was first applied, a broader and deeper mark was made. This script reached a syllabic and even a semi-alphabetic stage.

The Egyptians at a very early period began to use a picture script which became conventionalized thousands of years ago. This script went farther in its development than those described above, in that signs for separate letters came to be used. But the Egyptians continued to use with them the older signs, both syllabic and ideographic (*i.e.* picturing objects or thoughts). About three thousand hieroglyphic signs have been found, of which, however, only about three hundred are very common. The Egyptian hieroglyphics were not deciphered until one hundred years ago, when the then newly discovered Rosetta Stone, with its triple text — hieroglyphic, Coptic, and Greek — gave Champollion the key for which he was searching. Another script of pictographic origin is the Cretan, extensive records of which were found only a few years ago. A Champollion has not yet appeared to decipher this script for us.

II. THE ORIGIN OF
OUR ALPHABET

IT IS clear, as we shall see, that our present
script goes back, via Rome and Greece, to
the ancient Semites, though there is dispute about some of the details. The invention
of this alphabetic script was, as Renan said,
one of the greatest creations of the human
spirit. Roman writers tell us that the Semites
(or rather, more specifically, the Phoenician
Semites) obtained it from Egypt. In modern
times this tradition has at times been accepted,
at times rejected. An attempt was made by
the French scholar Rougé, whose results were
accepted and ably set forth by Isaac Taylor,
to show that the Semitic alphabet came from
an early form of Egyptian hieratic (a cursive
form of hieroglyphic). This theory is now
generally discredited. Sporadic attempts have
been made to derive the alphabet from cuneiform, from Cretan, and from various other
Mediterranean systems of writing, but none of
these has found wide acceptance.

It may occur to some that the Phoenicians developed their alphabet from a pictographic script of their own invention, but the fact that there are no traces of Phoenician pictographs is a conclusive proof that the Phoenician alphabet was based on the script of some other people. That script must have been one that was still pictographic in the third or second millennium B.C. The only script that seems to meet the requirements is the Egyptian, and Egypt, after all, was the natural place to look for this script. Recent discoveries have, as a matter of fact, made it very plausible that the alphabet was developed under Egyptian influence, though not in the way that Rougé thought.

In 1905 inscriptions were found in the Sinaitic peninsula, the full significance of which was not pointed out till 1916. The probable date of the inscriptions is about the nineteenth century B.C. The fact that out of 200 characters, there are not over twenty-five varieties, makes it seem that the script is alphabetic. That the language of the inscriptions is Semitic is now almost generally conceded, but they have not been interpreted to the satisfaction of all scholars. In these inscriptions there are several signs which bear a striking resemblance to characters in the oldest Semitic writing on the one hand, and to Egyptian hieroglyphics on the other. The oldest Semitic inscription of any extent known thus far was discovered in 1923 at the ancient Byblus (the Gebal of the Bible), Syria, in the tomb of King Ahiram. It has been assigned to the thirteenth century B.C. The oldest inscription the date of which is fixed by its contents is the Moabite stone of King Mesha. In this inscription the letter *aleph* (*a;* meaning " ox ") has a form easily derived from the character instantly recognized as the head of an ox found in the Sinai inscriptions. In Egyptian hieroglyphics the head of an ox is used to represent the word " ox." One very interesting thing is that the Sinai inscriptions have some characters more like those used in the South Semitic script than those of the North Semitic of the Byblus inscription and Moabite stone. This is true, for example, of the letter *pe* (*p;* meaning " mouth "). The explanation must be that the two branches of the Semitic were derived from an older common form of proto-Semitic. The old theory that the South Semitic alphabet was derived from the Phoenician must be abandoned.

In tracing the relation of the Semitic letters to the Egyptian hieroglyphs, we must start from the Semitic names of the letters. Most of them have clear and definite meanings. The Sinai inscriptions have removed all doubts as to the value of the names for finding the original forms of the letters. Only where the meaning of the letter is uncertain do we have difficulty in finding the appropriate Egyptian form.

In establishing the relation between Egyptian and Semitic, the crude Egyptian hieroglyphs found in Sinai furnish good transitional material. In their way they are quite as valuable as the Semitic inscriptions from Sinai.

Though it is likely that the Semitic alphabet was evolved from Egyptian hieroglyphs, it is in no sense true that our alphabet is of Egyptian origin. The hieroglyphs were merely convenient pictures of which some Semite made use. He did, however, get something more important from Egyptian script, the acrophonic principle. This means simply that the picture of a given object comes to be used as a permanent representation for the initial letter of the word for that object. So the plan of a house (a common Egyptian hieroglyph) came to represent the

[13]

letter *b* because that is the first letter of the Semitic word for house, *beth*.

It may be difficult for some to accept the theory that symbols were taken at random from the Egyptian script. But the older hypothesis of Rougé that the Semitic signs were taken from the Egyptian alphabetic signs which had the same value was quite as difficult, if we can put ourselves in the position of the ancient Semites and give up our feeling for the " naturalness " of expressing our words by alphabetic signs. The Egyptians themselves, as we have seen, had not progressed so far as to trust their alphabetic signs. Therefore, by way of example, the wavy line primarily represented " water," and only secondarily, the first letter of the word for water. In other words, Egyptian was still largely pictographic. It therefore was the natural thing for a Semite who wished to adapt the Egyptian symbols to his own language to take over the pictographic values, along with the acrophonic principle, and thus to say that the wavy line represented the first letter of the Semitic word for water (Hebrew *majim, mem*).

The time at which the Semitic alphabet was invented is a matter of dispute, but recent discoveries make it clear that we must attribute the

THE ORIGIN OF OUR ALPHABET

SINAI HIEROGLYPHIC	SINAI SEMITIC	BYBLUS XIII C.	MOAB IX C.	SOUTH SEMITIC	EARLY GREEK	HEBREW NAME	MEANING	GREEK NAME	ENGLISH
						aleph	ox	alpha	A
						beth	house	beta	B
						gimel	boomerang? camel?	gamma	C, G
						daleth	door	delta	D
						he (harm)	behold	e(psilon)	E
						vau	hook nail	(vau)	F, U, V, W, Y
						sayin	sickle weapon	zeta	Z
						cheth	fence	eta	H
						teth	basket?	theta	(Th)
						yod	hand	iota	I, J
						kaph	palm of hand	kappa	K
						lamed	cudgel ox-goad	lambda	L
						mem	water	mu	M
						nun (nahash)	fish (serpent)	nu	N
						samekh	prop	(xi)	(X)
						ayin	eye	o (micron)	O
						pe	mouth	pi	P
						tsade	side?	(san)	(S)
						qoph	knot	koppa	Q
						resh	head	rho	R
						shin	tooth	sigma	S
						tau	mark	tau	T

[15]

invention to an earlier period than used to be
assumed. If the Ahiram inscription really goes
back to the thirteenth century B.C., we must put
back the invention itself to a much earlier
period. The year 2000 B.C. is scarcely too
early and may even prove to be too late.[3] A
piece of pottery found at Gezer has three characters which were carved on it before the clay
was baked. It is thought to date from 2000–
1600 B.C. One character is the square form of
beth found at Sinai. Another looks like a hand
and may represent *kaph*. The Ahiram script
is later than the common ancestor of the North
and South Semitic scripts, though it clearly is
closer to that ancestor than the writing on the
Moabite stone. The forms of the *beth, he, vau,
cheth, lamed,* and *pe* are closer to the early
Greek alphabet than are the corresponding
forms of the Moabite stone. The South Semitic script must have split off from the main
branch several centuries before the Ahiram
script.

It may seem surprising that the Ahiram
script is not much more like that of the Sinai
inscriptions than is the Moabite script, which
is four centuries younger. The reasons are as
follows: the Sinai script is rough and unformed,

the other two are calligraphic; the Sinai script, even if we accept the earliest date suggested for it (nineteenth century B.C.), may be a case of arrested development, preserving a greater number of archaic features than the others.

What people shall have the credit for making the greatest contribution to our alphabet? That is an almost impossible matter to decide. Certainly the Egyptians contributed relatively little, as far as our present knowledge goes. The Semites, as the real inventors of the alphabet, contributed a great deal; yet, strictly speaking, Semitic script was not alphabetic; it was rather syllabic or semi-syllabic. There were no symbols for vowels, and the various characters represented consonants with or without following vowels, so that the reader had to supply the vowel which suited the context. It has been asserted that the alphabet was the invention of the Greeks but, important though their contribution was, as we shall see, such a statement is overdrawn, even if in a strict sense accurate. The Romans caused the alphabet to spread over most of the civilized world — and that is perhaps the greatest contribution of all. Certain it is that the writer, printer, and reader of this book owe most to the Romans.

It should be no surprise that the alphabet went through various stages of improvement as it passed from one people to another. The explanation is that the alphabet had to adapt itself to new conditions and that it found no barrier of conservative tradition among a people who had just adopted it. The result has been that the alphabet has tended to become universalized and more nearly perfect for world-wide use. This universalization, attained in the Roman period, together with the influence of the Roman Empire in spreading many phases of Roman civilization, is responsible for the present importance of Roman script. In this way we are justified in conceding to the Romans the leading position in the transmission of the alphabet.

The importance of the alphabet can be seen when we realize that it has had a strong restraining influence on the languages using it. The difficulty of distinguishing homonyms in alphabetic writing seems to have acted as a deterrent against producing them in large numbers. In languages which depend on other systems of writing, such as Chinese and Japanese, there is no such deterrent. It has also had a restraining influence on pronunciation, even in

English, in which the pronunciation has tended to run away from the spelling. It is impossible to imagine what the chief European languages of to-day would be like if they had adopted a system of writing like Chinese instead of an alphabetic script.

III. THE GREEK ALPHABET

THE SEMITIC origin of the Greek alphabet is beyond question. The resemblance of the letters of the early Greek inscriptions to those of the Byblus and other early Semitic monuments is striking. Besides, it is obvious that the Greek names of the letters were derived from the Semitic. As we have seen, these names have a significance in Semitic; in Greek, they have none. The order of the letters, which we know from very old Greek and Semitic sources, such as the alphabetic Psalms, is the same in Greek and Semitic. This order seems to be one of chance.

Ancient tradition, too, has it that the alphabet was brought to Greece by Phoenicians. The letters of the alphabet were often called " Phoenician " letters. The certainty as to their origin which we can reach without the tradition enables us to put confidence in other phases of the tradition.

An important question concerns the time when the Phoenician alphabet was introduced into Greece. The commonest tradition in antiquity was that the letters were brought by Cadmus of Tyre, who first went to the island of Thera, where he left some of his men and then proceeded to Boeotia, where he founded Thebes. This would take us back to the end of the fourteenth century B.C. — before the traditional date of the Trojan War (twelfth century). Now it is clear that the South Semitic script has some characteristics which show that it was derived from a script earlier than that of the Byblus inscription (thirteenth century). The earliest Greek alphabet has some resemblances to South Semitic as against North Semitic, especially in the form of lambda and sigma. Early Greek letters also agree better with those of the thirteenth-century Byblus inscription than with those of the ninth-century Moabite. Therefore it would seem necessary to assume that the Phoenician alphabet was brought to Greece some time before the thirteenth century B.C. — which brings us to the approximate date of Cadmus. Thus the alphabet was known to some of the Greeks at the time of the Trojan War. There is no reason why the Homeric poems could not have been penned when composed. The earliest extant

Greek inscriptions are at least as early as the eighth century B.C. and tradition speaks of still earlier ones.

Another phase of the tradition seems to be confirmed in striking fashion: it is precisely at Thera, where Cadmus is said to have landed first, that some of the oldest Greek inscriptions on Greek soil have been found. In these days when so many traditions about early Greek history are being confirmed by discoveries in Crete and in Asia Minor — the Cretan Labyrinth, the Achaeans, and Atreus are now vouched for — we may well be in a cordial mood toward the Cadmus story, even as to date. The best evidence as to the date of the Trojan War shows that it took place just about the time to which tradition assigns it.[4]

In the Semitic alphabet only consonantal sounds were recognized; vowels had to be supplied by the reader. We may compare some of our English abbreviations: *yr.* for *year, bldg.* for *building.* On account of a difference in language structure, Semitic perhaps did not suffer from ambiguity as a result of this limitation as much as some modern languages would. Somewhat parallel is the ambiguity in the case of Latin *levis.* Here the vowel sound of the

[22]

first syllable is represented by a character, to
be sure, but two different ways of pronouncing
that character produce two different words.

The greatest contribution of the Greeks was
the addition of vowels to the alphabet. This
was due in part to the prominent role played
by vowels in Greek, in part to the working of
the acrophonic principle. The Greeks in taking over the Semitic names of the letters naturally had difficulty with the pronunciation of
some which had no parallel in their own language. So the very first letter, *aleph,* was a
weak consonant unknown in Greek. In pronouncing the name, the Greeks simply omitted
the consonant, much as the cockney drops an
h, thereby exposing the following vowel sound,
which happened to be *a,* and thus the name and
value of alpha originated. Similarly the Semitic
he, a kind of aspirate, lost its initial sound when
pronounced by Greeks and took the value of
the vowel sound which followed it, namely *e*
(epsilon). The same thing happened again
with the consonant *ayin.* This might have become *a,* if *aleph* had not already usurped that
function. As it is, it received the value of *o*
(omicron). The vowel *i* (iota) was developed
in a different way. The Semitic *yod* was a semi-

vocalic consonant which easily became a vowel; compare the use of *i* in Latin as both vowel and consonant. As Greek no longer had the consonantal sound, iota was used only for the vowel. The vowel *u* (upsilon) in a similar way is a development of *vau* (digamma), a semivocalic consonant; compare again the use of *u* in Latin as both vowel and consonant. But in this case the Greeks needed the consonant as well as the vowel. Instead of using the same character for both, as the Romans did, they assigned to the vowel a *vau* of a slightly different shape and put it at the end of the alphabet as an added letter. This probably happened very soon after the introduction of the alphabet, as no Greek alphabet without upsilon has been discovered. Later on, it is curious to note, the *vau* (digamma[5]) ceased to be pronounced in the Eastern Greek and dropped out of the alphabet except as a numeral. If this had happened in early Greek before the introduction of the alphabet, the vowel *u* would come next to *e* in our alphabet.

The way in which the Greeks got their vowel symbols acted as a limitation on the number to be introduced. Under different conditions the Greeks might have developed at the outset more

than five characters for their vowel sounds, and
we might therefore have more than five vowels
in our modern alphabet. This limitation is the
chief weakness of the alphabet. The Ionic development of eta and of omega came too late to
affect the Latin alphabet and the modern alphabets derived from the Latin.

As we shall have occasion to see from time
to time, writing, like other human institutions,
reflects the character of peoples, even if it does
not reveal that of individuals, as some assert.
It is a familiar fact that the Greeks, in contrast to the Romans, failed to produce a united
nation. Athens did not succeed, as Rome did,
in becoming permanently supreme among the
city-states of its race. The same independence
is found in the script. Every city had its peculiarities. These have been broadly grouped
into two classes, Eastern and Western. The
latter includes Euboean towns (notably Chal-
cis), Boeotia, and part of the Peloponnesus and
their Italian and Sicilian colonies; the former,
Asia Minor, the Aegean islands, Attica, Corinth,
Argos, and their colonies. The distinction is
based on the difference in the letters added after
upsilon. In Western Greek the added letters
are X Φ Ψ, with the values xi, phi, chi; in

Eastern, Φ Χ Ψ, with the values phi, chi, psi.
The order and in part the values are different;
the original order seems to have been phi, chi,
xi. Probably the letters were invented in a
region using the Western alphabet. The name
of phi was made up on the analogy of pi, of
which it is merely an aspirated variant, and the
other letters (chi, xi, psi) followed this lead.
The forms of the new letters seem to be either
arbitrary changes of known letters or archaic
variants of them. So it seems almost certain
that Ψ (ψ) (Western chi) is an archaic kappa.

Eastern Greek in taking over these added letters confused their function and their order.
As a letter for *ks* had already been developed
out of the Semitic *samekh*, only the name xi was
adopted; the character Χ was made a chi. As
the Western chi (Ψ) was thus left without a
function, it was assigned a new value, *ps* (psi).

But these are not the only changes which
took place in Greek. A series of changes, not
yet satisfactorily explained, came about in the
adaptation of the Phoenician sibilants. Zeta
has the form and alphabetic position of *zayin*,
but its name seems to be derived from *tsade*.
Eastern Greek xi has the form and position of
samekh, but has a new name and function.

[26]

Certain Greek states had a letter san with the form of *tsade* and the name, apparently, of *shin*. Sigma preserves the form and position of *shin*, but the name of *samekh*.

The addition of vowels and other letters was not the only contribution which the Greeks made to alphabetic writing. They had a good deal to do, apparently, with determining the direction of writing. In the Egyptian hieroglyphs the writing is usually columnar, but sometimes in lines, more often from right to left than from left to right. The earliest Semitic seems to have used both directions. At least that appears to be the case in the early Semitic inscriptions from Sinai, as it certainly is in the later South Semitic inscriptions. In North Semitic, however, the direction of writing is regularly from right to left, a direction preserved in Hebrew as written to-day. Apparently the Greeks learned only this direction from the Phoenicians, since some of the earliest Greek inscriptions are written from right to left, as is true also of early Latin inscriptions. Yet it was not long before this method lost favor. At first we find a transitional phase in which the direction alternated from line to line. This the Greeks called *boustrophēdon,*

[27]

" ox turning," because they were reminded of oxen ploughing a furrow one way, then turning and ploughing the other way. One finds this in both Greek and Latin inscriptions. By the fifth century B.C. this method yielded to that in use at present, from left to right. Whether the Romans inherited all these methods from the Greeks and independently gave preference to our present method, or whether they imitated the changing Greek practice remains uncertain. At any rate, we owe to the Greeks and Romans this important simplification in writing; for to right-handed people it is much simpler to write from left to right. The change must have come about as a result of writing on papyrus and wax tablets, for in cutting inscriptions the direction is of slight importance. It may be pointed out that the early Greeks and Romans who could write *boustrophēdon* developed an ability that most of us lack to-day. As the direction of writing changed, the direction of certain asymmetrical letters, such as ᗺ and Ǝ, was changed, but symmetrical letters, such as O and T, were not affected.

As time went on, the Eastern and Western alphabets tended to become more and more differentiated, especially on account of changes in the former. These changes took place in the eighth century and later, chiefly in such Ionic cities of Asia Minor as Miletus, from which they gradually spread to the other districts in which the Eastern alphabet was used. The dropping of vau (digamma) has already been mentioned. Similarly, koppa gradually became obsolete and was retained only as a numeral. The acrophonic principle, whose influence has already been discussed, remained active: as heta tended to be pronounced eta, it lost its consonantal force and took the value of the exposed vowel, a long, open *e,* in contrast to the short, close sound of epsilon. It was probably after this development, though the converse is sometimes stated, that by analogy a separate character came to be used for a long, open *o* and to be placed at the end of the alphabet as omega. It is a differentiated form of omicron. This means, of course, that at an earlier period epsilon was used for both short and long sounds of *e* (also for *ei*) and omicron for both sounds of *o* (also for *ou*). Upsilon changed its pronunciation to that of modern French *u.*

See Plate I, *a.* Athens. Fifth century B.C. Note the use of H for *h,* XΣ for ξ and ΦΣ for ψ in χσυγ-

γραφ(σει), of Ο for ω in απομισθοσαι and for ου in
τος, of Ε for η in σκελε and for ει in οικοδομεσ(αι).
This illustration and the next are taken from Otto
Kern, *Inscriptiones Graecae*, Bonn, 1913, Nos. 14
and 44.

Another invention of those who used the
Eastern Greek alphabet was the doubling of
consonants. This began in the eighth century, apparently at Miletus. Before that time
consonants were doubled in speech, but not
in writing. The poet Ennius introduced this
practice into Latin in the second century B.C.,
and from Latin it has come into the modern
languages. As a result we have the curious
situation that in early Greek and Latin, consonants pronounced double were written single,
whereas in modern English they are written
double, but pronounced single. Italian is the
best example of a language which has the
doubled pronunciation.

The modifications made in the Eastern alphabet account for the chief differences between
it and the Latin alphabet which we use in English. Whether they are all desirable; whether,
in other words, the Eastern Greek alphabet
in its final form is a better alphabet than our
own, is an interesting question. Some of the

modifications, as the distinction of long and short *e* and *o*, are valuable; others, as the use of one character for two consonants in the case of *ps*, are superfluous.

By the fifth century the Ionic form of Eastern Greek was fully developed. In the course of its growth it gradually influenced the other Eastern Greek alphabets, in spite of the strong individualism of the Greek states. In 403 B.C. during the archonship of Euclides, the Ionic alphabet was officially adopted in Athens, the leading Greek state, though it had been in use there for some time before, especially in literary productions. Gradually the Ionic spread over the whole of Greece. This is essentially the alphabet which we know as the ancient Greek alphabet. Only the so-called capital letters were in use in ancient times; small letters are a mediaeval development.

See Plate I, *b*. Athens. Second century A.D.

IV. THE ITALIC ALPHABETS

IT IS clear that the various Italic dialects (Latin, Oscan, Umbrian, etc.) as well as Etruscan, which is still a language of mystery, received their alphabets from a Western Greek source. It is also clear that the Oscan and Umbrian alphabets were derived from the Etruscan. Differences between the Latin and Etruscan alphabets led to the view that the Romans borrowed their alphabet directly from the Greeks. But recent discoveries have brought about a modification of this view. There was an earlier and a later Etruscan alphabet. The Latin alphabet is descended from the former, the Oscan and Umbrian from the latter. This is more in accordance with what one would expect. For in its early days Rome's contact with Etruria was very close (witness the rule of the Tarquins during the sixth century, if tradition is right), and many of Rome's cultural borrowings from Greece were through the intermediation of Etruria.

The Western Greek source from which the

[32]

Etruscans borrowed their alphabet was, perhaps, the Chalcidian colony, Cumae, an ancient city near Naples. This is not certain,
however. The best example of the earliest
Etruscan alphabet is an abecedarium found a
few years ago at Marsiliana, near Orbetello. It
is one of the earliest examples of Greek writing we have, and the earliest abecedarium, dating from about 700 B.C. Inscribed on the ivory
edge of a wax tablet, it may have been used for
school purposes.

See Plate I, c. Marsiliana abecedarium (from
right to left).

The later Etruscan alphabet is chiefly characterized by a new letter in the shape of the
figure 8 with the value of f. The fact that a letter of this unusual shape is found also in Lydian
inscriptions has led some scholars to believe in
the truth of the ancient tradition that the Etruscans came from Lydia. But this letter is not
found in the earliest Etruscan, nor does the
Etruscan alphabet resemble the Lydian in other
respects. We have the choice of attributing the
identity of the unusual letters to coincidence,
or of explaining it as due to a late borrowing by
the Etruscans from the Lydians. If it is coin-

[33]

cidence, then the probable explanation of Etruscan 8 is that it is derived from the ⊟ (=h) of F⊟. In Latin F⊟ (found on the Praenestine fibula) was later reduced to F.

Just when the Romans obtained their alphabet is difficult to say. The oldest inscription (on the Praenestine fibula) probably dates from the seventh century, certainly not later than the sixth century, B.C. Another early inscription is in the Forum at Rome; it dates from the sixth century. Probably it was during the seventh century, when Etruria was dominant in Central Italy, that the alphabet was introduced.

See Plate II, *a*. Rome, Forum inscription. The writing is *boustrophedon;* reading up the right column, down the middle, and up the left: *quoiho| sakros es | ed sor.* Note the shapes of *q, h, r* and the variation in the direction of *e* to suit the direction of writing.

As may be seen from their inscriptions, the Etruscans made no use of B, D, O, X and only sparing use in the earlier period of K and Q. They used K only before *a* and Q only before *u,* a restriction which they had learned from the Greeks. In other positions C (at first the Greek gamma or *g*) was used for the sound *k;* later C alone was used for this sound. For the voiced palatal *g*, the Etruscans had no more need than for the other voiced mutes, *b* and *d*.

The early Etruscan abecedaria show, however, that the unused letters were not forgotten, and so it is that the Romans borrowed them along with the rest, for they had real need of them. But the original distinction between C and K had been lost sight of, and the Romans adopted the early Etruscan practice of limiting the use of the three identical consonants, C, K, Q to certain positions. The Latin names of these letters (*ce, ka, qu*) preserve this distinction. The sound of *g* as well as of *c* was expressed by the character C. Thus the Romans had three characters to express one sound (*k*), but no character to differentiate *g* from *k*. In the course of time they realized and corrected the difficulty. Strange to say, they did not assign the *k* function to the character K. The *k* sound had, in fact, taken such complete possession of the character C that the original and legitimate owner, *g*, was looked upon as the intruder and was made to find another home. Its new form is probably a C with a differentiating mark; the early form is G. It took as its place in the alphabet the one vacated by the Greek zeta, for which the Romans had no need. Another explanation derives G directly from zeta. The new letter first came into existence in the fourth or third century, but it was some time before its use was general. In the abbreviations C. (Gaius) and Cn. (Gnaeus) the older use of C for *g* was preserved throughout the Roman period. These names were always spelled with a G when written out, but never in abbreviation. There was no Latin word "Caius." Another abbreviation which preserves an old form is *M* (which we write M.'), standing for the praenomen Manius, which retains the original five-stroke *m*, and was used to differentiate from the abbreviation for Marcus. K eventually disappeared from the language, except as an abbreviation in a few words beginning with *ka* (*e.g. Kalendae*). But when the Roman alphabet was adopted by English and German, *k* again came into honor. And so we see that letters, like human beings, have their ups and downs.

Q was retained, but used only before *u;* eventually it was used only before consonantal *u,* that is, only when *u* was followed by another vowel. It is still employed in that way. Ever since that restriction was made, the *u* has been superfluous in writing, but in our conservatism we have failed to take even this slight step toward doing away with the superabundance of *k* sounds foisted upon the world by the Etruscans more than 2500 years ago. The famous orator Calvus, contemporary of Cicero and Caesar, refused to use the letter *q*. Nigidius Figulus, the learned grammarian of about the same period, did not use *q, k,* or *x.*[6] For some reason this excellent example did not meet with favor.

The Greek digamma was used with a following H in early Etruscan and in the earliest Latin to represent the sound of *f*. Later this was simplified by omission of the H. H retained its original sound as a consonant. The letter I, which as the Semitic *yod* shows, was originally a consonant and then in Greek became a vowel, returned in part to its original function as consonant, in part kept the Greek function as vowel. V retained its original vowel sound but, like I, also reverted to the consonantal value, since digamma or vau, originally the consonantal *u,* had taken on a new value. Other Western Greek letters (theta, phi, chi) used by the Etruscans, were not needed by the Romans and were therefore dropped, except as numerals, as we shall see later. It will be seen that in re-

[37]

taining F and Q and the original values of H and V, Latin was more conservative than Ionic Greek. The same is true of the shapes of some of the letters.

In Etruscan, Oscan, Umbrian, and Faliscan, the direction of writing is regularly from right to left. In the earliest Latin inscription, that on the Praenestine fibula, we find the same order. Later there occur some examples of *boustrophedon,* but almost from the first the Latin order is from left to right. Whether this was due to Greek influence or to native intelligence, it is a tribute to Roman common sense.

The developed alphabet of the Republic, including the new letter G, consisted of 21 letters, from A to X. During the last few centuries of the Republic, Rome had close contact with Greece and introduced a number of Greek words into its own language. For some of the Greek letters the Romans found no exact equivalents. This was true of the Greek upsilon, which had changed in sound from that of the corresponding Latin V (vowel) to that of the modern French *u.* At first they wrote *u* or *i* for it, but in the first century B.C., they introduced the upsilon in the shape then current and placed it at the end of the alphabet. Thus there were now three forms of the same original Semitic letter in the Latin alphabet: F, V, Y.

Similarly with zeta. The Romans had this letter in their alphabet at the outset, but soon discarded it because they had no use for it and gave its place to G.[7] When Greek words were introduced the need for a *z* was felt and accordingly Z was placed at the end of the alphabet. The letter *g* had been displaced by *c* and had in turn driven away *z*, which after a long absence had to be content with last place. Such is the struggle for existence. The Greek aspirates, Θ, Φ, X, were represented at first by T, P, C, later by TH, PH, CH. These led, therefore, to no additions to the alphabet.

Thus the complete Latin alphabet of 23 letters was formed. Attempts were made at various times to add new letters. The Emperor Claudius made an effort to add three more: an inverted F (Ⅎ) for consonantal *u*, ⊢ for the sound between *i* and *u*, Ɔ for *ps* and *bs*.[8] The first two are found in inscriptions of the period, but they did not survive; of the third no certain example has been found. The first of these was certainly meritorious, but Claudius was fifteen centuries ahead of his times, for it was not until the sixteenth century that our present distinction between the vowel *u* and the consonant *v* became fixed. May the emperor whose stupidity was made famous by Tacitus and Seneca have the satisfaction of knowing that his cleverness in at least one respect was so far in advance of his age!

As previously stated, the doubling of consonants was introduced by Ennius in the second century B.C., in imitation of Greek practice. A little later the poet Accius tried to distinguish long vowels from short by writing them double, but the innovation did not find favor.[9] If it had been successful, we should undoubtedly be using it to-day. By mere chance it happens that in English we use a double *e* with the value of long (English) *e: feed.* For a long time the Romans used a mark (*apex*) like an accent, made over long vowels except *i.* The long *i* was indicated by an *i* that was literally long, *i.e.* longer than the other letters in the line. But these methods did not survive antiquity.

V. THE DEVELOPMENT OF
THE LATIN ALPHABET

THE LETTERS of the Western Greek alphabet of course suffered changes in form as they passed via Cumae or some other Western Greek colony to Etruria and thence to Rome. During the thousand or more years between their introduction to Rome and the downfall of the Roman Empire further changes took place.

One important factor in altering the shapes of letters was the material on which they were used. From the earliest days of the alphabet stone and papyrus were the chief recipients of writing. Chiseling on stone naturally led to the use of straight lines, writing with pen and ink on papyrus led to the development of curves. But the two scripts tended to influence each other. As a result the history of alphabetic writing well down into Roman times reveals a pendulum swing which tends to settle down to a compromise between straight lines and curves, though the curves gradually have the better of

it. Even the earliest extant Phoenician inscriptions betray the influence of pen and ink writing. In the Roman period the same influence
continued.

The rounded B, C, D, P, R, S, all of which
may be paralleled in Greek, became the standard forms during the Roman Republic. Later,
as we shall see, the same tendency affected other
letters. On the other hand, the influence of
stone chiseling is seen in occasional examples
of the angular forms of these letters and even
of O and Q, which had always been curved.
But these angular shapes did not last.

Another element in the evolution of letters
was   the   tendency   towards   beautification
through regularity and symmetry. The letter
A is a good example. Closely related to this
tendency was the influence of one letter on another. The development of F was affected by
that of its neighbor E, Q by its near neighbor
O, M by its neighbor and relative N, G by its
cousin C — so much so that, as we saw, it is
hard to say whether G is a C with a distinguishing mark or a zeta affected by C. When P took
on a shape similar to that of its near neighbor
R, the latter received its distinguishing stroke,
and ever since the two have developed along

parallel lines. B too has been influenced by its cousin P, or perhaps the influence has been mutual. Nearness of position in the alphabet and similarity of sound value account for this interaction of one letter on another. The process is still going on. Environment as well as heredity has had its effect on the letters we use to-day. Indeed the process of evolution can be illustrated almost as well in the history of the alphabet as in the field of zoölogy. The creation of "sports" differing slightly from the typical forms is as characteristic a feature in the development of the letters of the alphabet as of animal or plant species. Numerous variants of the letters, some of them very strange and unusual, may be found in the records which have been preserved to us. But they have disappeared as a result of the operation of the law of the survival of the fittest. The chief factors which have tended to preserve certain forms as against others are implied in the foregoing account. The letter forms evolved by use of pen and ink have survived because they are more suited to the environment which has become typical of writing, *i.e.* writing material made of paper. The change from stone to papyrus, parchment, and paper may be compared to the environmental change from a cold to a warm climate. But the element of beauty is due, of course, to human choice, just as human choice has at times affected the development of species of plants and animals.

Still another factor bearing on the question of what form is fittest to survive is simplicity. A form that is hard to make because of a complicated series of lines yields to one whose lines are fewer or simpler. The same is true of a form that takes up a large amount of space. This is from the standpoint of the scribe, a consideration no longer of importance in this era of the printed book. From the point of view of the reader, the more legible form is more likely to survive. One or another of these factors exceeds the others in importance as conditions vary. Hence the alphabet has always been in a healthy state of growth.

As a result of all this, there was evolved during the last century of the Roman Republic a formal style of writing of a monumental character which remained the typical style of the Empire. This style is seen at its best in official inscriptions of the early Empire. At various periods in the later history of script, recourse has been had to this style as to a fountain-head of inspiration or, perhaps better, to a perfect model for what we now call capital letters. Even now this is true, with the result that the letters of a Roman inscription of the best period are as easily read as the capitals in a modern inscription or book.

See Plate II, *b*. Inscription found in the Largo Argentina at Rome. Time of Vespasian (first century A.D.). *c*. Inscription from a columbarium at Rome (*C. I. L.* VI. 5035). First century A.D.

VI. THE DEVELOPMENT OF
GREEK SCRIPT

BECAUSE of its lesser direct influence on our modern script we may make our survey of the development of Greek handwriting a hasty one before proceeding to a more leisurely and detailed discussion of Roman writing.

In an earlier chapter we noted that the Ionic form of the Eastern Greek alphabet was officially adopted by Athens in 403 B.C. From there it spread to the entire Greek world. The letter forms are essentially those of the capitals used to-day to reproduce ancient Greek.

Up to this point the history of the alphabet and writing has been based on the evidence of inscriptions on stone and metal for the simple reason that we have no documents written with pen and ink from the early period. The further history of inscriptional writing need not concern us here because it had no important influence on the history of writing in general and because we have available the much more valu-

[46]

able evidence of papyrus manuscripts for tracing the evolution of Greek writing. It is sufficient to point out that styles changed from
time to time and place to place.

See Plate III, *a*. Berlin, P. 9875. Fourth century
B.C. Timotheus, *Persae* 187–198: βασιλευς εις φυγην
ορμωντα παμμιγη στρατον γονυπετης αικιζε σωμα φατο δε
κυμαινων τυχαισιν Ιω κατασκαφαι δομων σειριαι τε ναες
Ελλανιδες αι κατα μεν ηλικα ωλεσατε ηβαν νεων πολυαν-
δρον ναες δε ουκι οπισσοπορευτον αξουσιμ πυρος δε αιθαλοεμ
μενος. This manuscript, published in 1903, is our only
source for the text. Note the form of ω. This illustration and the next two are taken from W. Schubart, *Papyri Graecae Berolinenses*, Bonn, 1911, Nos.
1, 4b, 19c.

The papyrus finds of Egypt have furnished
us with material for a study of Greek writing
from the fourth century B.C. to the eighth century A.D. Essentially there are two styles —
the literary book hand and the cursive hand of
everyday use. These interact on each other
from time to time. The book hand starts out
with a character very similar to that of the inscriptions, as may be seen from the fourth-cen-
tury manuscript of Timotheus. In the third
century, as a result no doubt of cursive influence, it becomes uncial, *i.e.* some of the letters
become rounded. First Σ becomes C; next E

[47]

becomes ϵ, and Ω becomes ω. Soon after we find Z for I and A for A, and this eventually becomes α. At the beginning of our era M has become μ, the typical later uncial form. Under obvious cursive influence the three-stroke Ξ becomes 3. Thus we see a gradually developing uncial script from the third century B.C. to the second century A.D.

See Plate III, *b*. Berlin, P. 9771. Third century B.C. Euripides, *Phaethon:* υπερ δε εμας κεφαλας πλεια μελπει δε δενδρεσι λεπταν αηδων αρομενα γοοις Ιτυν Ιτυν πολυθρηνον ριβαται κινουσι ποιμναν ελαται δ εις βοταναν ξανθαν . . .ων συζ | ται υπ ειρεσιαι. . . .αν αειραμενοι αχεουσιν. . . τνι αυ ακυμονι πομπαι σιγων. .ν ανεμων τε και φιλιας αλοχους σινδων δε π σομ πελαζει τα μ.ν ουν ετερων ετε κοσμειν υμεναι. . . . αει δεσπωσυν. Note the addition of δε above the line in vs. 2 and the forms of σ and ι (with a hook). *c.* Berlin, P. 6845. First or second century A.D. Homer, *Il.* VIII. 439‒443.

In the second and third centuries we find side by side with the broad uncial a sloping, compressed uncial, much as to-day we find vertical and slanting forms of writing side by side.

In the meantime there arose a cursive hand, used for business purposes, in which letters were written together instead of separately. This was at times written quite as carefully as the book hand, just as our cursive hand also has its regularized type form, called "script." The details of its evolution are of no interest to us here. It is sufficient to point out that the changes in the book hand were due to its influence. We can definitely say, for example, that the round alpha came into the book hand from the cursive, for it is found two centuries earlier in cursive than in the book hand. Similarly with other letters. It seems to be true that the chief borrowings from cursive came at two periods, one about 300 B.C., when Alexandria became the most important city of the Greek world, and the other nearly three hundred years later, when the Romans took over Egypt. It is natural that new political situations should affect the style of writing; history shows many such examples. To the earlier of these two periods we owe the forms ϵ, C, ω; to the latter, A and ɑ, ɯ, ξ. It is also worth noting that not all cursive forms affected the book hand, but those which did generally required a century or two to succeed. It is not impossible that Roman writing had an influence on both cursive and book hands in the earlier period as it surely did in the later.

The earliest Greek parchment manuscripts that have survived date from the third or fourth century A.D. They are written essentially in the uncial characters of the papyrus rolls. But the new material led to a differentiation in that it permitted the shading of letters to a much greater extent. It is true that some papyri show shading, but this probably is due to imitation of writing on parchment. The Ambrosian Homer of the third or fourth century is thought to be our earliest example of a parchment book. Other manuscripts of the fourth century are the Vatican and the Sinai Bibles; the Codex Alexandrinus is attributed to the following century.

See Plate IV, *a.* Rome, Vat. Gr. 1209, p. 672. Fourth century. *Psalm* 77. 8-12. Note the abbreviation of Θεοῦ in lines 1 and 6, the way *o* is crowded between τ and ν at the ends of lines 6 and 9, and the superposed corrections of τόξον to τόξοις (line 4), ἐπελάθεντο to ἐπελάθοντο (line 9), παιδίῳ to πεδίῳ (line 14). Accents and punctuation were added later.

The handsome, broad uncial, with its square and round letters, continued to be used until about the sixth century, and was contemporary with its Roman counterpart. But the sloping, compressed uncial found in the papyri was also used on parchment, though at first it was less common. The reason is obvious: it is a time-

and space-saving script, and in the earlier centuries, at least in Egypt, parchment was still the more expensive material and was used only when the saving of time and space was not a consideration. The most important early manuscript in sloping uncials is the Washington (Freer) manuscript of the Gospels, which is thought to have been written in the fourth century.[10] This style of writing eventually became the dominant type. It developed as its chief characteristic very heavy lines contrasted with fine ones and tended to become pointed, like the Gothic style of Roman writing. Upright forms with the same characteristics are also found. This type, which became common in the ninth century, is called Slavonic uncial because it formed the basis for the alphabet used in the Slavic languages. After that the uncial became more and more artificial. It lasted in an upright form until about the twelfth century.

See Plate IV, *b*. Washington, Freer collection, p. 372. Fourth century. Gospels, *Mark* 16. 18–20. Note the abbreviations of Κύριος Ἰησοῦς Χριστός (line 4), Θεοῦ (line 6), Κυρίου (line 7) and the stroke for *ν* above the last letters in lines 5 and 6. *c*. Rome, Vat. gr. 1666, f. 3r. Written in 800, probably at

[51]

Rome. Greek version of Gregory, *Dial.* I (Migne, *Pat. Lat.* 77, 150): σίας. Περὶ πολιτείας διαφόρων πατέρων τῶν ἐν τῇ Ἰταλείᾳ διαλαμψάντων. Βιβλίον α. Μιᾷ τῶν ἡμερῶν σφοδραῖς τισιν ἀνάγκαις κοσμικαῖς. Note the wrong accents in πολιτείας, Ἰταλείᾳ, Μίᾳ.

With the ninth century we come to a crossroads in the history of Greek writing. The main road of uncial goes on, but its traffic is that of the Slavic alphabet. The Greek traffic is diverted to a road that before crossing the main road was little known but now becomes the main highway for the Greek alphabet. That road, known as the cursive before it crosses the other highway, is the minuscule.

It is only necessary to examine the highly artificial uncial writing of the tenth or eleventh century to see that something was bound to happen. Writing such as this could not last. It is not surprising therefore that in the ninth century a minuscule style of writing based on the old cursive came into use as a formal book hand. This style of writing, called " old minuscule," is at its best in the ninth and tenth centuries. Though the letters are connected, there are no extreme ligatures; many of them involve the letter sigma. The letters are well rounded. In shape they are in general similar to modern

Greek minuscules, except beta, which is similar to our *u;* zeta, which is at first like our 3, later has the uncial Z form; eta, which is like our *h;* kappa, which looks like our *li* without a dot; nu, which is round at the bottom like a mu without the last stroke; pi, which has the form ϖ. The script may be compared in general with the Caroline minuscules of the Roman alphabet in the ninth and tenth centuries, to which it possibly owes its inspiration. The ninth century is noteworthy also because the use of accents and breathings becomes general, in both uncial and minuscule manuscripts.

See Plate V, *a*. Rome, Vat. gr. 190, f. 114v. Ninth century. Euclid VIII. I: Ἐὰν ὦσιν ὁσοιδη-ποτοῦν ἀριθμοὶ ἑξῆς ἀνάλογον· οἱ δὲ ἄκροι αὐτῶν πρῶτοι πρὸς ἀλλήλους ὦσιν, ἐλάχιστοι εἰσὶν τῶν τὸν αὐτὸν λόγον ἐχόντων αὐτοῖς· Ἔστωσαν ὁποσσοιοῦν ἀριθμοὶ ἑξῆς ἀνάλογον οἱ α β γ δ· οἱ δὲ ἄκροι αὐτῶν οἱ α δ πρῶ.

In the following centuries we find what is called the " middle minuscule," whose chief characteristic is the use of uncial forms of many letters, especially beta, eta, and kappa. We are on the way to a welding of uncial and minuscule scripts. At times it seems as if the result might be a cursive uncial. In fact uncial forms of every letter can be found in one or another manuscript of this period, but they are joined together in the cursive manner. Ligatures and abbreviations become more numerous.

See Plate V, *b*. New York, Pierpont Morgan Library, MS. 639, f. 294r. Twelfth century. Gospels, *Luke* 4. 16.

From the thirteenth century on we have preserved to us a number of more carelessly written manuscripts, filled with ligatures and abbreviations. In this respect the script recalls the contemporary Gothic of Western Europe, though in appearance they are quite unlike. Some letters have many shapes in the same manuscripts; most have at least two. It was a period of formlessness and carelessness, produced or at least assisted by political turmoil. Furthermore, the introduction of paper, the new cheap writing material, was responsible for a lesser degree of care in writing.

See Plate V, *c*. Rome, Vat. gr. 144, f. 1r. A.D. 1439. Cassius Dio 36. 1: καὶ ὅτι ἰσχυρα τῇ τύχη ἐπ' ἀμφότερα ἐκέχρητο ἐπέτρεψεν· ἡττηθείς τε γὰρ πολλὰ καὶ κρατήσας οὐκ ἐλάττω καὶ στρατηγικώτερος ἀπ' αὐτῶν ἐπεπίστευτο γεγονέναι. αὐτοί τε οὖν ὡς καὶ τότε πρῶτον ἀρχόμενοι τοῦ πολέμου παρεσκευάζοντο καὶ πρὸς τοὺς περιχώρους τούς τε ἄλλους καὶ 'Αρσάκην τὸν Πάρθον καίπερ· ἐχθρὸν τῷ Τιγράνη διὰ χώραν τινὰ ἀμφισβητήσιμον ὄντα ἐπρεσβεύοντο· καὶ ταύτης τε αὐτῷ ἀφίσταντο καὶ τοὺς Ῥωμαίους διέβαλλον λέγοντες ὅτι ἂν μονωθέν-των σφῶν κρατήσωσι καὶ. Iota subscript is not indicated.

With the reawakening of interest in Greek in fifteenth-century Italy, Greek scholars and scribes came to Italy, especially after the fall of Constantinople in 1453. Naturally they brought with them the undesirable writing then current. It was at this unfortunate time that printing began, and the early Greek books printed in Italy preserve all the numerous ligatures and other peculiarities of this writing. In the course of centuries the printed forms gradually became simplified under the influence of the Roman script, but it was not until the nineteenth century that all ligatures disappeared. Even so the present printed form of Greek is less beautiful and less legible than Roman type. As Rutherford said: "Nothing could well be imagined less likely to call up ideas of art or beauty than a modern page of printed Greek." [11] Very recently there have been suggestions in Greece that the Greek alphabet be abandoned in favor of the Roman for the printed and written forms of modern Greek. Unfortunately it is unlikely by reason of national pride that this movement will make much headway. Curiously enough

the cursive script of Greece was reformed during the nineteenth century on the model of the
slanting style at that time in vogue in Western
Europe and is therefore much more Roman (*e.g.*
in the beta) than the printed type fonts. It
would be helpful if the Roman forms were used
at least for those letters which correspond ex-
actly and in the case of which no ambiguity
would result.

As for the printing of ancient Greek for the
use of non-Greeks, there certainly is no good
reason for not using Roman types. At times attempts have been made to improve the Greek
type fonts but without much success. A few
years ago a rather handsome font was designed
by a committee of the Hellenic Society of England,[12] but apparently it has met with little or
no success. An earlier design has had only
slight vogue.[11]

We may conclude this chapter with a discussion of some alphabets derived from the Greek.
The Copts of Egypt in the early centuries of
our era abandoned their own cumbersome
script, descended from hieroglyphs, in favor of
the Greek uncial letters then current in their
country, supplementing these with seven characters taken from their original script.

[56]

In the ninth century the Bulgarians adapted the current Greek minuscule to the writing of their language. That is, they accepted the minuscule forms of the letters but did not connect them in cursive form. They added a number of characters based on Greek ligatures. This script is called Glagolitic, and was current in Bulgaria and Croatia. There are manuscripts in existence as old as the tenth and eleventh centuries. This form of script came into use in the Eastern Orthodox Church, in the writing of the language known as Old Church Slavonic (*i.e.* Old Bulgarian), and spread with it. At the same time another script was introduced, based on the ninth- and tenth-century uncials that, as we saw, are called Slavonic because of their use as a base for the Slavic alphabet. This second script, called Cyrillic, did not come into general use for several centuries, after the Glagolitic had developed complicated forms. At first the Cyrillic may have been used as a sort of majuscule script for special purposes. The Cyrillic too needed additional characters; these it took in part from Greek ligatures, in part from the Glagolitic alphabet. The new alphabet spread throughout the Eastern Slavic territory, wherever the Orthodox

Church is dominant, *i.e.* Jugoslavia, Bulgaria, Russia. Roman Catholic Slavs use the Latin alphabet. The Glagolitic maintained itself in general use among the Croats until the seventeenth century. Modern Russian is a form of Cyrillic modified and simplified in the time of Peter the Great. As in the case of modern Greek, the Russian cursive script reveals greater influence on the part of the Roman writing of Western Europe than the printed type does.

The early Germanic runes were at one time thought to be derived from Latin and Greek, but a more plausible explanation has recently been given, that they were derived from very early North Italian alphabets akin to but essentially independent of the Latin alphabet. This explanation accounts for the similarities to both Latin and Greek.[13]

The alphabet devised by Ulfilas in the fourth century A.D. for his translation of the Bible into Gothic was based on Greek uncials, with some borrowings from Latin and the runes.

VII. THE WRITING OF THE ROMAN EMPIRE

THE SQUARE capitals of the Roman inscriptions were also used in formal books written on papyrus and parchment down to the fifth century A.D. Examples of this script on parchment are found only in two fragments, both of which are of Virgil manuscripts — notably the one now partly in the Vatican (3256) and partly in Berlin (lat. fol. 416) and known as the Augusteus because it was once thought to have been written in the age of Augustus. It is now usually dated as fourth or fifth century. Fragments of a Virgil at St. Gall (1394) in palimpsest may belong to the fourth century. There are also papyrus fragments of a Virgil from Oxyrhynchus. In this script the letters have the monumental and geometrical appearance familiar from inscriptions. The straight lines are really straight and are usually horizontal or vertical. The O and Q tend to be perfect circles, and C and G are arcs of a circle. But the influence of writing with a slanted pen is shown in the tilted O and in the strong shading of the oblique stroke of N. This strong shading is general and is produced by the flat side of a broad pen. The earliest examples of such shading are in inscriptions of the Augustan Age, which presuppose a still earlier use in writing with a pen. Some of the letters have finishing strokes, or serifs, as they still do in our writing. These are found in Latin inscriptions as early as the second century B.C.; in Greek inscriptions they occur even earlier. Only F and L project slightly above the line, and the tail of the Q is below, but this is not enough to change the cast of the writing. The letters are written in the main between two lines, which is the distinguishing characteristic of majuscule script, in contrast with minuscules, which, because of the letters projecting above and below, are written between four lines: B D P Q b d p q.

See Plate VI, *a*. Rome, Vat. lat. 3256, f. 4r. Square capitals. Virgil, *Georg*. I. 253–256. The "Augusteus" of Virgil. At the ends of the lines the letters are smaller so that the lines may not run over. In line 1 *que* is abbreviated.

Rustic capitals are a somewhat less stiff form of majuscule writing. They reveal to a greater extent the influence of pen and ink on papyrus or parchment. It is true that they are also found in inscriptions, but this is due to imitation of pen and ink writing. Besides fragments of about twenty manuscripts we have four more or less complete manuscripts of Virgil (Vat. 3225, 3867, Pal. 1631; Florence, Laur. 39. 1) and one of Terence, called Bembinus (Vat. 3226), of the fourth and fifth centuries. The script was in use much earlier; we have papyrus fragments and inscriptions from the first century.

See Plate VI, *b*. Rome, Vat. lat. 3225, f. 64r. Rustic capitals. Virgil, *Aen*. VII. 302–305. The punctuation was added later. The first letter of the page (shown here) is somewhat larger.

In comparing this script with the square capitals we note that the letters are compressed; thus O and Q are no longer circles but have elliptical form. Straight lines tend to curve, as in A, X, and V; the latter has indeed become a U. The ends of lines do not always meet, as we note in the case of A and M; the former is well on the way to the shape of our modern small a. Serifs are not as common or regular but sometimes more prominent, especially in

[61]

A, P, and T. Because of the short cross stroke at the top and the long finishing stroke at the bottom the T looks like an I. More letters dip below the line, *e.g.* N and V.

The abbreviations in both kinds of capital script are discussed elsewhere (Chapter XV). Here we merely need to note that at first the horizontal abbreviation sign was used for *n* and *m*. Later a distinction was made by putting a dot under the stroke to indicate *m*. A ligature of NT (in the form N̄) and occasionally of other letters was permitted at the end of a line. Words were generally written continuously without space between them.

Of almost thirty complete or fragmentary manuscripts in square or rustic capitals only two are Christian — a Prudentius and a Sedulius. Only a few pagés of the latter are in rustic capitals, the rest, significantly enough, in uncials. Prudentius was the Christian Virgil and received the special honor of being treated, in this manuscript, like Virgil. It may be said then that square and rustic capitals were employed almost exclusively for *de luxe* copies of the pagan authors and that the use of square capitals persisted especially to honor Virgil.

Thus far we have been discussing the formal

script of the early centuries of our era. There was also the much less formal writing to be found in letters, business papers, documents, etc. This form of writing was characterized by its tendency to keep pen on papyrus without removing it. Thus it has been given the name of *cursive,* "running," just as our writing is cursive as compared with printing. Naturally there was much variation, depending on the haste, care, or experience of the writer. Ligatures were numerous.

The material for the study of cursive writing consists of papyrus documents and letters found in Egypt (which, however, do not begin to compare in amount with the Greek documents), *graffiti* scratched in the stucco walls of Pompeii, inscriptions painted on these same walls, such as election posters and announcements of gladiatorial contests, and wax tablets found at Pompeii and in Dacia.

The earliest examples of cursive show striking deviations from the formal capitals in use at the same time, but in comparison with later cursive the earlier style is distinctly closer to capitals. It is therefore sometimes called majuscule cursive in contrast to the later minuscule cursive. Yet minuscule characteristics manifest themselves very early: letters extend above and below the line more frequently and more decidedly, in true minuscule fashion. Letter forms that we are accustomed to call minuscule make their appearance. In fact, the beginning of nearly all our minuscule forms may be found in the cursive writing of the first three centuries.

The cursive script becomes increasingly important on account of its influence on the formal book hand. Thus it affected first the uncial hand. The name " uncial " means " inch high " and is an exaggerated term used by St. Jerome for the large size letters found in *de luxe* books but applied specifically in modern times to a variety of majuscule script. It has been extended also to the formal Greek writing in use from the third century B.C. to the twelfth century A.D., as we have seen in Chapter VI. Our earliest Roman uncial manuscripts belong to the fourth century, but the script must have been used earlier, as there are examples in inscriptions of the third century.

The most characteristic letters of uncial writing are ᶛ , ᶁ, ϵ, ᶆ — suggesting that we can remember the writing as the " adem " script. Perhaps we might even so name it instead of using the meaningless term "uncial." The *h* and *q* have taken on our minuscule form. The curving forms of these letters clearly indicate their origin in the use of pen and ink and in the desire to make letters in the fewest possible strokes. Thus the *e* can be made in two strokes instead of the four required for the capital E, though it will be noted that once a script is formalized, as is true of uncial writing, this advantage is given up. Thus it costs the scribe only one less stroke to make the uncial ɱ (three) than the capital M.

The new shapes of the letters are due to cursive influence. In the Vercelli Gospels, thought to date from about A.D. 371 and to be our oldest example of uncial writing, the *a* is without a loop, as in our earliest cursive writing. The initial stages of the looped *a* are found in papyri of the second century and the finished form in the fourth. Uncial forms of *d, e, h* are found in the cursive writing of the first century of our era — the earliest that is preserved to us. Cursive forms of *m* which suggest the uncial *m* are also found in that century, though they are not so close in shape. The uncial *m*, even in its earliest examples, has an individuality which suggests a fairly long period of independent development. It should be remembered that we think of uncial script only in its fully developed book form, chiefly because of the lack of earlier less formal material. But both the material we have and the analogy of Greek writing show that the uncial is the crystallized form of a script which experimented with cursive forms. Thus a third-century inscription from Africa [14] has uncial forms of *a* (fully developed), *d, e,* but still preserves the capital *m.* On the other hand, it has the minuscule *b* in a form rarely found in papyri before the fourth century. Another inscription, also from Africa, has a good example of uncial *m.*[15] Our discussion of the relation of cursive and uncial will be resumed when we come to the half-uncial script.

See Plate VI, *c.* Rome, Vat. lat. 5757, p. 254. Palimpsest; both scripts are uncial. Augustine, *Enarr. in Psalm.* cxxxviii, 31 (VII–VIII century) over Cicero, *De rep.* V. 5. The latter reads: *p(ublicam) et in ea quo|dam modo | vilicare pos|sit summi iu| nim illis ad ar|tem suam u|titur sed se | a suo mune.*

Uncial letters, especially in the later period, go above and below the main lines of script more freely than capitals, but not enough to take them out of the majuscule class. Abbreviations and ligatures are similar to those in capital writing. In the ecclesiastical works the *nomina sacra* are in contracted form.

Well over four hundred manuscripts and fragments of uncial written between the fourth and eighth centuries have been preserved to us. Of these 390 have been listed.[16] The great bulk of them are biblical, patristic, or mediaeval. Virgil, represented by the only manuscripts in square capitals left to us and by four in rustic capitals, is not found at all in uncial form. In fact, only one classical poem (Ovid, *Ex Ponto*) is preserved in this script. This fact alone was enough to cast suspicion on the forged fragment of Catullus published a few years ago.[17] Of prose writers Cicero is represented six times, and the *scholia* on his speeches once. Livy is represented seven times; Pliny the Elder, six times; Fronto, once; Hyginus, once; Granius Licinianus, once. We may now add the Morgan copy of Pliny's *Letters*. There are also a number of fourth- and fifth-century writers on technical subjects such as geography, medicine, law, grammar. The interest in Pliny the Elder was largely medical. The legal writers include a few earlier ones like Ulpian and Gaius. The collection of writers on surveying was put together in the sixth century, though it contains

[67]

some earlier works. The Latin Anthology was assembled at the same time and in similar fashion.

See Plate VII, *a*. New York, Pierpont Morgan Library, MS. 462, f. 6v. Uncial, about A.D. 500. Pliny, *Epist*. II. 4. 7–8. The correction in line 2 is of about the same period.

On the other hand, we have no copy of the Bible in capitals, either square or rustic, and almost no Christian work. It is obvious that the uncial script was in a peculiar sense a Christian development. The hand was formalized by the early copyists of the Bible. In doing this they may well have been influenced by the uncials then current in the Greek Bibles, just as they were in the writing of the *nomina sacra* (Chapter XV). It is interesting to note that besides Bibles several of the Latin uncial books are Greek-Latin glossaries and others are translations from the Greek. At any rate, the later uncial script shows decided Greek influence. Early uncial is distinguished chiefly by the shape of *e* and *m*. The former is almost like the minuscule letter, as in our printed form, though the loop is not quite closed; *m* has a straight first stroke, or at least one that does not turn in at the bottom. In both letters the early uncial is more like the cursive. In late uncial both letters become symmetrical and artificial: the cross stroke of the *e* is in the exact center of the arc, and the first and last strokes of the *m* curve inward in identical fashion. This symmetry characterizes Greek uncial as early as the fourth century. The late uncial *e* of Latin is similar to the Greek epsilon. Latin *m* did not imitate Greek mu because that letter had developed along different lines; rather it was influenced, at least indirectly, by omega. In some manuscripts omega is almost closed at the top and looks very much like Latin uncial *m*. The same principle of symmetry appears in other late Latin uncials. Thus *o* at first is shaded in an unbalanced way, with heavy lines at the lower left and the upper right; this was due to writing in the natural way with the pen slanting. Later the heaviness is centered right and left, owing to a more artificial way of writing with the pen held straight. The same is true of Greek omicron. Compare also sigma and *c*. Also the later Latin *t* has a long cross stroke like the Greek tau.[18]

See Plate VII, *b*. New York, Pierpont Morgan Library, MS. 334. Uncial, A.D. 669. Augustine, *In Epist. Ioh. ad Parth. Tract.* VI. 3 (Migne, *Pat.*

Lat. 35, 2021): *per cupiditatem mundi multa mira faciunt sinistra operatur non dextera. Dextra debet operari et nesciente sinistra ut nec misceat se cupiditas saeculi quando.*

Of course it may be held that these are independent developments in Latin and Greek. But the fact that the Latin uncial script is so predominantly ecclesiastical ties it up with the Greek, much in the same way as the use of *nomina sacra* in contraction shows Greek influence. The interaction of Greek and Roman writing on each other from the earliest times down to the present deserves further study.

Among the best-known uncial manuscripts are the Vercelli Gospels (written about A.D. 371), Cicero, *De re publica* (palimpsest; Vat. 5757), Scholia Bobiensia on Cicero's *Orations* (Vat. 5750, Milan, Ambr. E. 147 sup.), Livy, third decade (Paris 5730), Livy, fifth decade (Vienna 15), Jerome's *Chronicle* (Oxford, Bodl. Auct. T. 2.26), Fulda Gospels, Codex Amiatinus of the Bible (Florence, Laur. Am. 1), the Morgan fragments of Pliny's *Letters*, Verona Gaius.

Uncial writing as such did not have much influence on the forms of writing which succeeded it nor has it been resorted to in modern times to any great extent. It did maintain itself for a time in headings and titles, as we use capitals. The *a* passed into the minuscule hand and is still used in our lower case roman type. The uncial *d* was also used in later minuscule but has disappeared from our type fonts. Uncial forms of *e, d,* or *m* are now occasionally used for ornamental purposes.

The importance of cursive writing in its effect on the book hand has already been pointed out. As a matter of fact the development of the cursive hand in the first four centuries of our era is definitely responsible for the origin not only of uncials as distinguished from capitals but also of the minuscule hands of the Middle Ages and to-day. It should be remembered that the formalized book hands went on with relatively little change until they decayed, while the ever young and vital cursive grew this way and that. By the fourth century the cursive had developed a decidedly minuscule cast, and most of its letters had attained the form of the later minuscules. This writing is the cursive ancestor of mediaeval and modern minuscule writing.

See Plate VII, *c.* Strasbourg, Pap. lat. 1. Cursive, fourth century. Letter of recommendation: *refi-*

centiae tuae traduntur quod honeste respicere velit 'non dubito domine praedicabilis quapropter theofanen oriundum ex civitate hermupolitanorum provinciae thebaidos qui ex suggestione domini mei fratris nostri. The illustration is taken from *Archiv für Papyrusforschung*, III (1904).

It is unfortunate that the terminology and classification of Latin writing was fixed at a time when the papyri of Egypt and the *graffiti* and other cursive materials of Pompeii were still unknown. We have found it difficult to readjust ourselves to the facts brought to light by the new material. Let us think of uncial as a book hand which developed out of capitals under cursive influence. Let us remember further that this particular formalization is only one of many that might have taken place. The newer finds in Egypt in fact tell us that there were many incipient hands which might have developed into book scripts. These differ in the extent and nature of the cursive influence. Some have minuscule letter forms, not found in what we call uncial. The name mixed uncials has been applied to them — unfortunately, because it implies that they originated in uncials. We ought rather to say that these scripts and uncials both originated in the same kind of mixture of capital and cursive letters. The only difference is that uncials, as a result of some special influence, or perhaps pure accident, early developed into a widely used book hand, while the others did not, with one exception that we shall note. One of these so-called mixed uncials is probably earlier in date than any uncials left to us. That is the fragment of the Epitome of Livy (Oxyrhynchus 668) assigned by some to the third century, though others put it in the fourth. This manuscript has minuscule forms of *b*, *d*, *m*, and *r*. Other letters are the same in form as those in uncial writing but should not be called uncial — in part they are capital, such as N, in part they are cursive, such as *a* and *e*. In fact the long center stroke of the *e*, regularly striking the following letter, clearly shows its cursive origin, for in cursive this stroke is the one which connects the *e* with the next letter. There are, it is true, some late manuscripts which are mixed uncials in the proper sense of the term, *i.e.* they are uncials with an admixture of cursive forms. Even some clearly uncial manuscripts have occasional cursive forms in addition to the regular ones. Such forms

[73]

usually occur at or near the end of a line, when
space can be gained by using a narrower cursive letter.

See Plate VIII, *a.* Manchester, John Rylands
Library, Pap. 61. "Mixed" uncial, fifth century.
Cicero, *Cat.* II. 15. A papyrus fragment from
Egypt. The Latin is in the left column and a
word for word Greek translation in the right — a
kind of "Loeb translation" for those who knew
little Latin but much Greek: *belli | ac nefarii | pe-
riculum | depellatur | dicatur sane.* πολεμου | και αθε-
μιτου | ο κινδυνος | απωθηθειη | λεχθησεται μαλιστα.
From the *New Paleographical Society*, Series II,
Part III, 55.

The term half-uncial is sometimes used
loosely for mixed uncials of the type described,
but in a narrower sense it is applied to a very
definite script that became a rival of uncial as
a book script from the fifth to the eighth centuries. Again the name is unfortunate in its
suggestion that it was derived from uncial.
Rather it is a younger brother of that script,
making use of an almost complete minuscule
alphabet. It does not use the shapes of *a, d, e,
m* characteristic of uncial script but rather
those of modern minuscule type, except that
the *a* is in the form used in italics, not roman.
The only letter which maintains its capital

form is N, and this letter readily enables one to distinguish this script from later minuscules. The reason for the preservation of this kind of N was to avoid confusion with the minuscule *r*, which in some half-uncials is very much like *n*. The desire to avoid ambiguity is seen also in the *b*, which is in the form familiar to-day instead of the form like *d* which was the commonest type in the cursive of the first four centuries. The uncial influence is seen in the artificial writing with a straight pen (*e.g.* in the symmetrical *o*) in the later examples.

See Plate VIII, *c*. Rome, Vat. Reg. lat. 886, f. 97v. Half-uncial, sixth century. Theodosian, *Cod*. X, 10, 27, 1: *fuerit institutum sibi integri anni spatium recognoscat idoneum satis tempus muniendae congruae tractatibus litis et instruendi quem deserit laris habiturus nec ad iactu.*

There is difference of opinion whether one should speak of half-uncials as minuscules or majuscules. Like so many other controversies, this one is due to variation in definition and use of words. If by minuscules we mean letters which are clearly to be written between four lines instead of two, then half-uncials are minuscule. The same is true if we test this writing by the shapes of the letters or their relatively smaller size. If we mean by minuscule a script which is used in the body of the text while another style is used for running heads, then both uncials and half-uncials are minuscule, for in uncial manuscripts we find running heads in rustic or square capitals, and uncial titles are found in half-uncial manuscripts. It is true that in later times half-uncial was thought of as a script suitable for titles for a minuscule text, but that does not make it majuscule any more than lower-case italics or black-face letters are majuscules when we use them in headings. The difficulty is that extreme forms of majuscules and minuscules are easily distinguished while intermediate forms are not.

Lowe lists 160 half-uncial manuscripts [19] but includes a number that may be called mixed uncials. In fact all the fragments from Egypt (seventeen) seem to belong to this class. We may examine the list from another point of view. The older classical literature is strongly represented in the Egyptian mixed uncials. There are also three examples of mixed uncials in the marginal notes found in one uncial and two rustic manuscripts of classical works. Only one classical author (Juvenal, in the Ambrosian Library, Milan) is found in standard half-uncials.

There are a few legal and other late works written in this script, but for the most part the books are ecclesiastical or mediaeval. Thus the standard half-uncial, like the uncial, was a script selected by Christian scribes from among many formalized cursive scripts. Probably each was developed first at some particular center of writing.

Among the important early specimens of half-uncial are a Hilary (Rome, St. Peter's D. 182) written in 509–510 or shortly before, a Sulpicius Severus (Verona xxxviii, 36) written in 517, a pseudo-Ambrosius (Monte Cassino 150) written in 570 or shortly before, and a Eugippius (Vatican 3375) of slightly later date.

One of the characteristic features of cursive writing was the use of ligatures. These were used very sparingly in capital and uncial writing but they become much more frequent in half-uncial. Among them was the ligature for *et*, already found in cursive, which persisted throughout later periods. Another common feature of the half-uncial was the use of ę for *ae*. This cursive element, found occasionally even in uncial, continued in use until modern times.

As we survey the writing of the Roman Empire we find at the outset two types, the formal hand which was preserved on monuments of stone but also imitated on papyrus and parchment, and the cursive hand of informal writing. The book hands of the Empire other than the square capital are the product of the mating of the monumental with the cursive script. Their earliest offspring to achieve fame, Rustic, takes after its stiff and formal father, Square Capital, rather than after mother Cursive. The second child which grew up and prospered was Uncial, and he showed greater resemblance to his mother than his elder brother did. There were many other children of this curiously matched couple — the stiff, pompous father Capital and the quick, lively, rather slatternly mother Cursive, but all of them died during infancy or childhood except one, Half-Uncial. This child grew up and became famous. It took after its mother rather than its father but was like its father in showing more concern about its personal appearance. And that is the early history of this family during the Roman Empire. How the couple later separated and how the members of the family went their own ways is a story that belongs to the Middle Ages.

VIII. THE NATIONAL HANDS OF THE EARLY MIDDLE AGES

THE DEVELOPMENT of Roman writing closely parallels that of the Latin language. The formal style of Latin literature has kinship with the formal book hand in which it was preserved. Both are the products of professionals. The informal, even vulgar, speech of daily life suggests cursive writing. Colloquial forms such as *sodes* for *si audes* may in a way be compared to the ligatures of cursive.

But in the course of time formal Latin felt the influence of the vulgar speech just as formal writing felt that of the cursive script. Thus the literary language of the fourth and fifth centuries may be compared to the rustic capitals and uncials of that period. Occasionally the vulgar elements predominate even in more or less literary works, such as the *Peregrinatio* of Saint Aetheria (Silvia). In script we have the analogy of the half-uncial, in which cursive elements play a major role.

With the coming of the Germanic invaders in the fifth century Italy and Rome gradually became separated from the provinces. Without the unifying effect of the Roman army and the Roman government the vulgar forms of the language and the script gradually got the upper hand. In the transitional centuries, from about the sixth to the eighth, the formal Latin language maintained itself in the written records, though under the surface the vulgar speech in different regions was getting farther and farther away from the Latin of Rome and from that of other localities and was preparing for its ultimate triumph. So uncial and half-uncial writing continued to be used in books but the cursive hand was actively developing along lines of its own in the various countries of the former Roman Empire. The vulgar form of Gallic Latin emerges as a separate written language, French, in the ninth century; in Italy and Spain the process was perhaps slower, to judge merely from actual survivals. In script the development was more rapid: national scripts began to emerge as early as the seventh century. Thereafter the analogy between language and script in large part disappears. The nationalistic tendency of language increased and that of script decreased. By the time that the various languages had won established positions the doom of the national hands was already certain.

But there is a further analogy between language and writing which must be mentioned. From time to time the various Romance languages have borrowed words from Latin literature — " book " words they are called. So too the national hands borrowed from the old Latin scripts, capital, uncial, half-uncial. Furthermore the Romance languages have continually borrowed from one another. Similarly the national hands were influenced in their development by one another.

It has often been pointed out that when a radical gets into power he becomes conservative. The case of writing is not dissimilar. Half-uncial arose as a sort of radical protest against capital and uncial. But in the end half-uncials became as formal and conservative as uncials. They became enamored of the frock coat and the high hat, so to speak. It was time for the cursive lower class to raise another of its sons to power.

The development of the national scripts in the seventh century coincides with the real beginning of mediaevalism. Pope Gregory I,

who died in 604, has been called the first mediaeval man. Education ceased to be secular
and became wholly ecclesiastical. Pagan learning all but disappeared. Curiously enough it
flourished most in the extreme western outpost
of Roman civilization — Ireland. Here too the
classical half-uncial continued to be written,
though in modified form. From Ireland the all
but dying sparks of interest in pagan literature
spread to England and eventually to the Continent, where they joined the kindling flames that
burst into the mighty fire of the Carolingian
Renaissance.

1. INSULAR SCRIPT

IN THE island of Britain the Latin language
and writing practically disappeared soon after
the coming of the Germanic Angles, Saxons,
and Jutes in the fifth century. For such writing as these people did they used the runes
which they brought with them (page 58).
But in the sixth century Latin writing was re-
introduced into England by Augustine and his
monks when they came to convert the island to
Christianity. The Christianization of Ireland,
begun in the fourth century, was completed in
the fifth by St. Patrick. The language of Chris-

tianity was formal, not vulgar, Latin, and the writing was the formal uncial and half-uncial, not the cursive. Thus the national hand of England and Ireland, which we call Insular, was developed, not from cursive, as were the Continental hands, but from half-uncial, under the influence of uncial. At least that is the origin of the Irish style, which in the seventh century spread first to the north and then to the south of England and stopped the independent development of the uncial writing introduced there by the first missionaries from Rome.

As early as the seventh century, from which our oldest specimens date, the Irish script has easily distinguished peculiarities. Two styles developed, a formal, broad type known as the round hand, and a compressed type known as pointed. The round hand disappeared in both Ireland and England in the ninth century; the pointed lasted longer.

Among the famous early examples of the round hand are the seventh-century Book of Kells, an Irish manuscript of the Gospels, and the Lindisfarne Gospels written in England about A.D. 700. The most noticeable characteristic is the peculiar thickening of the tops or first strokes of letters. This is triangular in shape and reminds one of cuneiform writing. Another characteristic is the curving of *l* and *b*. This similarity of *b* and *l* is a marked peculiarity. The shading is very heavy. Following the half-uncial style on which it was modelled and the late uncial which it imitated the writing was done largely with a straight pen. Hence the symmetrical *o* and other peculiarities. Uncial as well as half-uncial forms of *a, d, r, s* are found. The *n* is sometimes minuscule. The use of elaborate tracery of a peculiar type, especially in initials, is a marked characteristic. In general the English examples carry these characteristics to greater extremes.

See Plate IX, *a*. Rome, Vat. Barb. lat. 570, f. 32r. Round Insular (Anglo-Saxon), eighth century. Evangelistary, *Matth*. II. 18. 16: *lucratus es fratrem tuum. Si autem te non audierit adhibe tecum adhuc unum vel duos ut in ore duorum testium vel trium stet omne verbum. Quod si non audierit eos dic aeclesiae. Si autem aeclesiam non au.* Note the abbreviation for *autem* (like an *h* with a hook), the double abbreviation stroke for *m*, and the characteristic decoration with dots.

Much more common than the round hand was the pointed, which has continued in use until the present day in the writing of Gaelic.

This was much less formal than the round hand. Being written more rapidly and taking less room, it may in a sense be compared with cursive. It is sometimes called minuscule by those who call the round hand majuscule or half-uncial. The letters are long and narrow instead of short and fat. The thickening of initial strokes is often found in the pointed as in the round hand, but the main strokes taper off into points, thus giving still more the suggestion of cuneiform writing. There is a tendency toward angularity adumbrated even in the round hand. In the pointed hand *r* tends to look like *n* but is differentiated either by lengthening the first stroke or shortening the second or bending it to the right. Sometimes *r* and *s* are much alike on account of the prominent initial stroke of the *s*. There is an open *p* which is sometimes confused with the long *r*. The half-uncial *g* (something like the figure 5) is characteristic of both round and pointed styles. The earliest examples are usually put in the eighth century, though the beginning of the development may be seen in the seventh. The first dated copy is the Book of Armagh (A.D. 807). The Berne Horace belongs to the ninth century.

[85]

See Plate IX, *b*. London, Brit. Mus. Cotton Tiber. C. II. Pointed Insular, eighth century. Bede, *Hist. Eccl.* V. I: *Vir venerabilis Oidilunald qui multis annis in monasterio quod dicitur Inhrypum acceptum presbyteratus officium condignis gradu ipse.* Note the ligatures of *en, er, st, ep, es.*

Three of the old runes were preserved in the writing of Anglo-Saxon: edh, an uncial *d* with a line through it for *th;* thorn, developed from a *d* and also having the value of *th;* and wyn (wen), used for *w*. The edh disappeared and the wyn yielded to *w*, which is actually a " double u " (or *v*). The thorn (þ) eventually came to look like *y* and disappeared, except in the form *ye* for *the*, as in " ye editor," " ye olde tavern." In such expressions *ye* has no relation to the pronoun *ye*.

Ligatures are so common in Insular script as to indicate cursive influence or cursive experience. Especially frequent are the ligatures of a tall *e* with a following letter and of an *i* extending below the line with a preceding letter. There is also a tendency to write letters in ligature below the line, as in the old cursive.

But the most interesting characteristic of Insular writing is the use of numerous abbreviations. These were derived from the Tironian

[86]

Notes and the *notae iuris*. Among them are
ʰ for *autem* (often mistaken for *hoc* by Continental scribes), ÷ for *est*, 7 for *et*, Ɔ for
con, ꝫ for *eius*, ł for *vel*, ƕ for *enim*, ṁ for *mihi*,
ꝑ for *per*, ꝗ for *quia*, ꝙ for *quod*, ţ for *tibi*.
Chiefly confined to the Irish are a̅n̅ for *ante*, g̊
for *ergo*, nł for *nihil*, n̊ for *nisi*, and many others.

In the tenth century the Carolingian hand
of France supplanted the pointed hand of England in the writing of Latin while Anglo-Saxon
continued to be written in the pointed style,
though this too was influenced by the Carolingian. The two hands were even used side
by side in the same manuscript for the two languages. The pointed hand might well have
lasted indefinitely, as it did in Ireland, if it
had not been for the Norman Conquest. After
the eleventh century this hand disappears from
England.

The Insular hand was written not only in
Ireland and England but also on the Continent
as a consequence of the missionary activity of
Irish and English monks. The Irish founded
monasteries or in other ways brought their
culture and writing to France (Luxeuil, Corbie,
Reims), Germany (Würzburg, Cologne, Rei-
chenau), Switzerland (St. Gall), and Italy

[87]

(Bobbio) in the late sixth and the seventh centuries, and the Anglo-Saxons did the same in the eighth (Fulda, Hersfeld, Lorsch, Echternach, Mainz). Though the Insular hand did not last long in the Continental centers, it did affect the writing at these places and contributed to the evolution of the Carolingian hand. Alcuin, the Englishman from York, had something to do with that development, as we shall see. But the greatest and most enduring contribution of Insular to the Continental script was its system of abbreviation, inherited from ancient sources which had in large part been neglected by Continental scribes.

See Plate IX, *c*. New York, Academy of Medicine (formerly Phillipps 275), f. 7v. Carolingian and Continental Insular, ninth century, probably from Fulda. Apicius, II. 1. 1–3. Carolingian and Insular alternate in the manuscript. In this illustration *farcimina* is Carolingian, the rest Insular: *Isicia fiunt marina de cammaris et astacis de lolligine de sepia de lucusta. Esicum condies pipere ligustico cumino laseris radice esicia de lolligine sublatis crinibus in fulmento tundes sicuti adsolet pulma et in mortario et in liquamine diligenter frigatur et ex inde esicia plassantur esicia.* Photograph from Dr. Margaret B. Wilson, donor of the manuscript.

2. THE VISIGOTHIC SCRIPT

THE HANDWRITING of Spain is known as Visigothic, though it has nothing whatever to do with the Visigoths except that it developed after their conquest of Spain. Its contemporary name was *littera Toletana* — Toledo script. It has a history similar to that of South Italian writing: it grew out of the cursive and was permitted to develop along its own lines for a long time, until in the twelfth century French writing, introduced in particular by the monks of Cluny, supplanted it. The Visigothic did not attain as much individualism as the Beneventan of Southern Italy; it is less easy to distinguish at a glance. Its best period is the tenth century, when the letters are firm and round; later they become pointed. The writing is compact and usually without much shading. In early examples the letters slant backward.

The special characteristic of Visigothic is the uncial *g*, with a prolonged tail. It resembles a figure 9, usually with a straight tail. As this form is found in Spanish half-uncial, it probably came into the national hand from that source rather than directly from uncial. This is but one evidence of half-uncial influence on

this script. The loop of *g* is open, to distinguish
it from *q*. The writer of that day had to mind
his *g*'s and *q*'s. Other paired letters besides *g*
and *q* are *a* and *u,* tall *i* and *l, r* and *s*. Tall *i*
and *a* are distinguished from *l* and *u* respectively by a curving last line, whereas that of *l*
and *u* is vertical. Sometimes the first stroke of
a has a pronounced curve, causing the letter to
resemble a joined *ci*. *I* is regularly tall at the
beginning of a word unless it is followed by a
tall letter, and even then tall *i* may be used;
within a word it occurs between vowels. Thus
we find *In, Iam, ille* or *Ille, eIus*. The letters *r*
and *s* are differentiated in that *s* is not joined
to a following letter. Even when *r* is not in
ligature it has a connecting stroke turning up-
ward. Both the uncial and minuscule forms of
d are used. The *t* is similar to that of Beneventan: the cross stroke makes a complete curve
down at the left and touches the upright. The
y is tall like our capital form.

Numerous ligatures were inherited from cursive, though the extreme forms tend to disappear in the course of time. An *a* shaped like an
epsilon occurs both in and above the line. A
v-shaped *u* occurs above the line, though not in
ligature. A ligature of *it* consists of an exten-

sion of an *i* into a *t;* it has the appearance of a long *t.*

Spanish abbreviations have distinct peculiarities. Most characteristic is a combined suspension and contraction in which vowels are suppressed and the consonants, or most of them, retained; thus we have a return to the original Semitic alphabet. Examples are *dmns* for *dominus, apstls* or *apsls* for *apostolus, epscps* or *epscs* for *episcopus, nsr, nsi,* etc., for *noster, nostri,* etc. The abbreviation stroke is used. Other Spanish abbreviations are *aum* for *autem,* ₚP for *per* (in other scripts it stands for *pro*), ꝗ for *qui* (in other scripts this represents *quod*). For *is* a hook or cedilla is used below *b* and *l.* The distinction between the abbreviation strokes for *m* and *n* found in some capitals and uncials is frequently found in Visigothic: *m* is represented by ∸, *n* by — . Both are also used as general abbreviation strokes.

See Plate VIII, *b.* Rome, Vat. Reg. lat. 708, f. 3v. Visigothic, eleventh century. Isidore, *Sent.* I. 10–11 (Migne, *Pat. Lat.* 83, 578): *Sicut lex et gratia, sicut initium et profectio, sicut bonum et melius. Kaput. Lex divina in tribus distinguitur partibus, idest in hystoria, in preceptis, et in prophetiis. Ystoria est in his que gesta sunt, precepta, in his que*

[91]

iussa sunt, profetia. Note the characteristically Spanish abbreviation of *sicut.*

Another peculiarity of Spanish manuscripts, though it is not strictly a matter of writing, is the spelling of certain Latin words. Thus the spellings *quum* (for the conjunction *cum*) and *quur* (for *cur*) in early manuscripts is considered a Spanish " symptom." Likewise *mici* (*mihi*), *nicil* (*nihil*). These are really examples of the dropping of *h*, as they stand for *michi* and *nichil*. In general *h* is often omitted or added in the wrong place. Prosthetic *i* is common (*iscribo* for *scribo*), as is the opposite fault of dropping an *i* (*stius* for *istius*).

An important criterion in dating Spanish manuscripts is the treatment of assibilated *ti*, before a vowel. About the year 900 this begins to be differentiated from the unassibilated form by prolonging the *i* and often turning it to the left. In the tenth century the tall letters become taller and have little ticks at the top.

Few manuscripts of classical Latin authors in Visigothic script are known to exist to-day. There is a Terence in Madrid (Hh74). An Ausonius in Leiden (Voss. lat. 111) is in Visigothic but was probably written at Lyons.

3. NORTH ITALIAN AND BENEVENTAN SCRIPTS

THE SEVENTH century marks the end of ancient and the beginning of mediaeval Italy. The new order, which made itself felt in every phase of life, was due to the invasion of the Lombards and the growth of the papal power. The invaders ran through the center of Italy but eventually became separated into two groups, the northern, including what we now know as Lombardy and much more, and the southern, covering the duchies of Spoleto and Benevento. The two groups were kept apart by the papacy, which gradually increased its power between Rome and Ravenna, and as a consequence each went its own way.

We have manuscripts of the seventh and eighth centuries which were written in Northern Italy in a formalized cursive or a mixture of cursive and half-uncial or uncial. The earliest examples are naturally very similar to the cursive of documents. Ligatures are numerous. One or more standard scripts might have been developed if the Carolingian hand had not taken the field in the ninth century. Even before this the pre-Carolingian hands of France

[93]

exerted an influence in Northern Italy, so that some scholars treat the North Italian scripts as members of the group of French scripts out of which Carolingian grew. The more important centers were Verona, Vercelli, Lucca, and Bobbio. From Lucca we have a famous manuscript containing Jerome's *Chronicle,* the *Liber Pontificalis,* and other works. It was written just before and after the year 800 by about forty scribes in almost all the styles of writing then known, including that of Spain. Bobbio was founded in 614 by the Irish monk Columban and was the center of influence of Insular on Italian script.

See Plate X, *a.* Rome, Vat. lat. 5763, f. 47r. North Italian (Bobbio), eighth century. Isidore, *Etym.* III, *Praef.: quantibus disciplinis de mathematica. Mathematica latine dicitur doctrinalis scientia quae abstractam considerat quantitatem. Abstracta enim quantitas est quam intellectum a materia separantes aut ab aliis accedentibus.* The *m* of *intellectum* was deleted and expunged. The script is still full of cursive ligatures.

In Southern Italy the independent growth of the cursive was not affected by the Carolingian reform for many centuries, for this part of Italy remained isolated. Even Charle-

magne could not secure more than nominal suze-
rainty over it, and after his time not even that
was admitted. Hence there developed a peculiar style of writing that used to be called
Lombardic but is now generally named Beneventan, from the duchy rather than the city of
Benevento. " South Italian " would be a less
misleading name. Its chief center was the
Old Benedictine monastery of Monte Cassino.
This script also spread to Dalmatia.

The earliest examples of South Italian writing are not essentially different from those of
North Italy. Beginning with the ninth century we find examples which, in the light of our
knowledge of the perfected Beneventan type,
we can recognize as first steps. Tenth-century
examples are definitely Beneventan, but the
perfection of the form does not come until the
eleventh and twelfth centuries. The decline
and fall of the script take place in the late
twelfth and thirteenth centuries. It is one of
the most individual and highly formalized of
all the varieties of Roman writing.

It will serve our purpose to describe the
style at its best. The writing is heavily shaded,
and the general effect is that of a downward
movement slanting to the right. This is par-

ticularly noticeable in the late degraded examples, in which the letters do not stand out so
distinctly and one gets a general picture of the
page without noting the individual letters. As a
result of this characteristic the script looks
broken and in fact is. Hence the name " broken
Lombardic." This peculiarity is especially
marked in the letters *i, u, m, n.* Each stroke
is made in two parts. In the letters which
have rounded parts the movement down to the
right is also noteworthy. The naturalness of
this in writing with a slanted pen is shown by
its use in uncials. Even the long letters, written vertically, harmonize with the others. Thus
the tops of the tall letters often are knobs made
by a short stroke written downward to the right.
The letters that go below the line have descend-
ers whose right edges are shorter than their
left, *i.e.* they are bevelled off.

The script has a close-joined appearance.
This is due to three factors. In the first place
many ligatures inherited from cursive were
carefully preserved. So we find a long *i* regularly in ligature after *e, f, g, l, r, t* and occasionally after other letters. The letters *p, r, t* are
also sometimes joined in ligature with preceding letters. With a following letter we find *a*

(*ae*) and *t*. The *ti* ligature has two forms, carefully differentiated. For the unassibilated sound the regular *t* is used with a lengthened *i;* in other words, the *i* is in ligature with the preceding *t*. In assibilated *ti* both letters have special forms, and the combination resembles a reversed *β*: *ᛏ*. The upper loop is really the cross stroke of the *t* continued downward to form the *i*. The cursive ligature form of *e,* with a broken back (*ℓ*) is used exclusively even when there is no ligature. Sometimes a double or broken *c* symmetrical with *e* is used. The long *r* developed in ligatures eventually became the regular form everywhere. The ligatures with *i* were so regular a part of the script that correctors often changed untied forms to tied, just as the proofreader to-day changes *fi* printed as two letters to the ligature *fi*.

See Plate X, *b*. Rome, Vat. lat. 3539, f. 21v. Beneventan, end of eleventh century. Sulpicius Severus, *Dial.* I (II. 1–2): *sequebamur. Interim ei seminudus hibernis mensibus pauper occurrit. Orans sibi vestimentum dari. Tunc ille accersito archidiacono iussit algentem sine. Mensibus* is in erasure. At the left is part of a large illuminated initial *q*.

A second factor in giving the script the appearance of closeness is the form of the connecting stroke of some letters. This is horizontal and comes at the top of the main line of writing. Its great regularity and prominence often give the impression of a continuous straight line at the top of the short letters.

Third in bringing the letters together is a sort of combination which has, somewhat unfortunately, been called " union." This ties letters together more closely than connecting strokes do but less than ligatures. It consists of joining round letters in such a way that the heavy strokes come in contact. In Beneventan this is not carried as far as in Gothic, for the letters merely touch without fusing.

The most characteristic letter of Beneventan is *a,* shaped at first like *cc,* later like *oc* joined together. In this form it looks very much like the distinctive *t* of this script. The *d* has the minuscule form at first but later the uncial, which fits better into the oblique cast of the script. The *r* is highly individual. It consists of a straight line extending slightly above and below the line, with a knobbed shoulder and a horizontal connecting stroke.

See Plate X, *c.*   Rome, Vat. lat. 3327, f. 36v. Beneventan (Bari type, used also in Dalmatia), twelfth or thirteenth century.   Sallust, *Iug.* I. 3-4.

At the left is part of a large illuminated *f*. The abbreviations include those for *que, eripere cuiquam, cupidinibus, pessumdatus est, usus, nature.*

The most typical abbreviation of Beneventan is that for *eius: ei* in ligature with a horizontal stroke through the bottom of the *i*. In general, abbreviation is by suspension and contraction. In the course of time abbreviations are sparingly introduced from Insular and other sources.

Criteria for dating Beneventan manuscripts are implicit in the description just given. A clearly recognizable Beneventan cast points to the tenth century or later. Absolute regularity and artificiality coupled with strength and beauty are found in the eleventh and twelfth centuries. Angularity and a degree of illegibility are characteristic of the thirteenth century. Indiscriminate use of uncial *a* suggests a late date; presence of the minuscule *d* makes for an early one. Before the eleventh century final *r* is regularly short; thereafter it is apt to be long, as it is in other parts of a word. The frequent use of the round *r* (like our figure 2) is a sign of lateness. Strokes over *ii* begin in the eleventh century; over a single *i*, in the thirteenth. Hyphens are not found before the

twelfth century. The presence of certain abbreviations points to a late date. The syllable
tur is abbreviated by *t* with a horizontal line
above it until the tenth century; in the latter
part of the tenth and the early eleventh an apostrophe is substituted for the line, thereafter a
sign shaped like a 2 is used. Abbreviation by
use of superscript letters begins in the eleventh
century.

Several famous manuscripts of classical authors are in Beneventan script, *e.g.* Florence,
Laur. 68.2 of the eleventh century, the one
manuscript of value for the text of Tacitus' *His-
tories* (i–v) and *Annals* (xi–xvi) as well as
Apuleius' *Metamorphoses* and *Florida*. Varro's
De Lingua Latina is known only from a Beneventan manuscript, Florence, Laur. 51.10
(eleventh century), and its copies.

4. THE MEROVINGIAN OR PRE-CAROLINGIAN SCRIPT

IT HAS been customary to speak of the early
hand of France as Merovingian, from the name
of the dynasty which was nominally in power
during most of its existence. As a matter of
fact there were various Merovingian hands

which we are beginning to distinguish, just as there were various dialects in the language.

In recent years the term pre-Carolingian has become a familiar one to describe the scripts current in France and Northern Italy just before the Carolingian style developed. It is a rather unfortunate term. Insular, Merovingian, and Beneventan are pre-Carolingian in the sense that they were used in their respective territories before the coming of Carolingian. The term pre-Carolingian is, of course, applied to various scripts to indicate that Carolingian grew out of them. On this principle the eighth-century writing of Southern Italy may with perfect justice be called pre-Beneventan.

The earliest examples of Merovingian are decidedly cursive, with many ligatures, and the shapes of the letters are often determined by the necessity for ligature. The most characteristic letter is *a*, which has many forms. The open *a* is very common and looks like *u*, being differentiated only by its final stroke being turned to the right to join the next letter, whereas *u* is never so joined. In some scripts both strokes of the *a* curve to the right, so that it looks like *cc*. Sometimes the *a* is closed but it is then usually wider than our italic *a*. The

[101]

uncial *a* also appears occasionally. The *d* is usually cursive; the loop is often open because of connection with a preceding letter, and the long stroke goes below the line. The *o* often has one or two connecting strokes at the top. The cross-stroke of the *t* turns down at the left, sometimes forming a loop. Beginning with the eighth century abbreviations become frequent, probably as a result of Insular influence.

In the Luxeuil type of the seventh and eighth centuries we have a decidedly cursive script very similar to that used in the legal documents of the time. In spite of the numerous ligatures there is an attempt to formalize the script so as to harmonize with the uncials and half-uncials used in headings and other special matter. The characteristic open *a* is bent back and consists of two identical strokes close together, each of which is divided into three parts: ⋘. Luxeuil in particular and Burgundy in general played a large part in the development of pre-Carolingian script.

See Plate XI, *a*. London, Brit. Mus. 29972, f. 35v. Luxeuil script, eighth century. Old Testament, *Wisdom of Solomon*, 13. 11–14, beginning *cem et arte sua usus diligenter fabricet vas utile in conversationem vitae Reliquias autem eius operis ad praeparationem escae abutatur et reliquum horum quod.*

A number of types originated or were used in the important center of Corbie, in Northern France, founded by monks from Luxeuil. The az type, assigned by some to Laon, was employed and may have originated at Corbie. It has an *a* consisting of two angular *c*'s: ⟪. The *z* is high and decidedly cursive: Ⅶ. Ligatures are rather common. This script may be derived from the Luxeuil type.

Better known is the ab type used at Corbie in the eighth and ninth centuries. Here the *a* looks like ic (without a dot). The *b* has a very small loop and in keeping with its cursive origin a horizontal line above the loop to connect with the following letter: ƀ. On the other hand the roundness of the letters shows the half-uncial influence.

Another Corbie script has been named the en type, a not altogether happy name because the *n* has no individuality but is merely the capital form borrowed from half-uncial. Another indication of the influence of half-uncial on this script is the reduction in the number of ligatures. The letter most prominent in ligature is a peculiar *e*, closed or almost closed at the bottom and provided with a hook ranging to the right.

Other types betray a still greater degree of half-uncial and even uncial influence. Thus the Corbie script which has been called the Leutchar type (Leutchar was abbot of Corbie in the eighth century) avoids ligatures, has a broad, round appearance instead of the cramped look of cursive, and employs the half-uncial N and the uncial G. Indeed some call it a half-uncial script.

In the meantime half-uncial was being written at centers like Tours and was being influenced by cursive writing.

IX. THE CAROLINGIAN SCRIPT

THE TERM Carolingian, or Caroline, rests on the belief that the script sprang full-grown from the brain of Charlemagne, with Alcuin standing by as midwife. But as we no longer believe in the old myths, there is now rather general agreement that Caroline was the child of Father Half-Uncial and Mother Cursive. Yet this agreement has produced a hot controversy: does Caroline take after her mother or her father? There are those who say that she is the very image of her father and shows the effect of her father's long residence at Tours. Others again argue that the mother's influence is paramount. They have in mind some of the older brothers and sisters of Caroline, not so famous as she, who took after their mother. Among them were the Corbie brothers, ab and en. We must remember that Caroline's looks changed from time to time. At Tours, her father's home, she presented a handsome appearance and was her

father's child. Then too, as she grew older she
gave up some of the idiosyncrasies inherited
from her mother. We must not forget more-
over that Half-Uncial belonged to the same
family as Cursive and that their child was
bound to resemble them both. Furthermore
the genetic experts see minute resemblances to
the mother which the ordinary person over-
looks.

But putting aside this extended figurative
language, so reminiscent of mediaeval allegory,
let us consider what we mean by Carolingian
and how it came into being. When we look at
a good specimen of this writing and compare
it with seventh-century Merovingian, we have
no difficulty in seeing that this is a different
script. Yet Carolingian was not a wonderful
new invention suddenly brought to the notice
of a startled world. It was rather a gradual
development that many persons no doubt failed
to note. Even the finished Carolingian form
did not remain constant but continued developing. The fact is that in many centers there was
formalization of the cursive scripts under the
influence of half-uncial and sometimes uncial
and Insular. Those scripts which were least
influenced by the half-uncial did not survive.

[106]

Nor was the new script a deliberate revival of half-uncial. Yet as we compare Carolingian with earlier writing it resembles nothing so much as good half-uncial. In fact the uninitiated have trouble in differentiating the two. As far as the development of writing is concerned it perhaps is of little importance whether Carolingian developed out of cursive under half-uncial influence, or whether the roles of these two scripts should be interchanged, but from the standpoint of the history of culture it is interesting to know whether Carolingian is a debased half-uncial or a cursive which has climbed to higher levels. The latter view is favored by the history of the Romance languages and by the parallel development of half-uncial out of cursive, not out of uncial, as we saw in an earlier chapter.

By the year 780 there had emerged at Corbie a type (called Maurdramnus after the abbot of that name) which is essentially Carolingian. It is used side by side with the more cursive ab type. In some respects (as in the use of uncial a) it is more advanced than many ninth-century examples of Carolingian. Its most prominent peculiarity is the unusually heavy dot or knob with which the *f* and *s* begin: **ſ**.

This is probably a mere exaggeration of a cursive trait, though it may be an outgrowth of Insular split *f* and *s* (p. 85).

See Plate XI, *b.* Leningrad Q. I. 16, f. 81v. "Maurdramnus" script, eighth century. Jerome, *Liber comitis* (Migne, *Pat. Lat.* 30, 519 D), quoting *Acts* 10. 37–38. The title reads: *Feria II ad sanctum Petrum. Lectio actuum.* The first line of the text is in half-uncial. The abbreviations are to be expanded thus: *fratres, per, Iesum, Nazareth, eum deus spiritu sancto et.* From *Palaeographia Latina,* I, Plate V (1922).

At the same time several manuscripts in an early Carolingian type were being written in what has been called the court school (*schola Palatina*), which accompanied Charlemagne on his travels but had its permanent home at Aix. These are the Godesscalc Evangelistary, written between 781 and 783 at Charlemagne's order and now at Paris; the Dagolf Psalter, presented by Charlemagne to Pope Hadrian I in 795, now at Vienna; and the famous Ada Gospels at Treves.

The question arises whether the script of these manuscripts of the court school was influenced by Charlemagne or Alcuin. At the most we may say that they may have encouraged this style of writing; it was invented by neither of them. The same question arises concerning the *ne plus ultra* of Carolingian writing that was perfected at Tours by the middle of the ninth century. Since Alcuin was abbot of the monastery of St. Martin's at Tours from 796 to 804, it used to be thought that, under Charlemagne's patronage, he was responsible for the Tours script. More recently this view has been rejected. At the best Alcuin could merely have encouraged the continuance of a system already in vogue. The correct answer to the question may be found when we answer a larger question: was Charlemagne the cause or the effect of the political and cultural progress of his time? The answer is that the movements which started in the seventh and eighth centuries happened to culminate in his time. The confusion caused by the Germanic invasions had passed away, and Germanic and Roman elements had fused and produced a new culture. The work of the Irish and English missionaries and teachers had its effect. Education, interest in learning, religious enthusiasm had spread. The loyalty of these missionaries to the Church at Rome brought together Church and State; the crowning of Charlemagne by

Pope Leo III as emperor and Augustus in 800 was the natural result. And in a sense he was a new Augustus, one who consolidated the achievements of his predecessors and encouraged culture in every field. The increased interest in culture led to the copying of more manuscripts, especially of the classics, and thus to the advancement of writing.

There are those who deny that any existing manuscripts written in the " regular " style of Tours, *i.e.* the characteristic Tours style with cursive elements all but eliminated, date from the time of Alcuin, and that Alcuin had any part in its development.[20] Others believe that several manuscripts written in this style date from Alcuin's time and that he was responsible at least for the encouragement of this script, though they admit that most of the examples, as well as those of the still better, " perfected " style, were written after Alcuin's death.[21]

It is time to ask ourselves what the characteristics of the Carolingian script are. It is sometimes spoken of as the first real minuscule, but this is a misapprehension or a misuse of terms, as already noted (p. 75). Its resemblance to half-uncial has been pointed out. The chief differences are in the shapes of some letters, though even here the differences are not constant. The capital N characteristic of half-uncial is found occasionally in early Caroline minuscule, but the small *n* is the usual form. The 5-shaped *g* of half-uncial is not used; instead we find the minuscule *g*. At first the two loops tend to be open, and the letter looks like the figure 3; later the top loop closes, then the bottom, and the letter approximates its modern form. A preponderance of open *a*'s indicates a ninth-century manuscript, as a rule. Later the uncial *a* (found as early as the eighth century) becomes the accepted form and has remained so to this day. It was introduced to avoid the confusions caused by cursive *a*, especially with *u*. Uncial *d* (ꝺ) is also found early and gradually becomes common. Occasionally a tall *c* is found.

Regular and symmetrical clubbing of the tall letters, a relic of the loop stage of cursive, becomes a characteristic feature. In the tenth century this begins to disappear. The letters are shaded but not excessively.

See Plate XII, *a*. Rome, Vat. Reg. lat. 762, f. 32r. Tours, before A.D. 820. Livy, XXII. 61. 10–11.

This script has been called "improved cursive." The text of this manuscript is here quite different from that adopted by editors.

As compared with Merovingian, the Carolingian has far fewer ligatures, but they do not disappear entirely. The tendency to eliminate ligatures was particularly strong at Tours, where the influence of half-uncial was so effective, and there are manuscripts of Tours written in the early ninth century which are without them. But this example did not prevail either at Tours or elsewhere. Most common is the *et* ligature. The diphthong *ae* is frequently written ҽ, sometimes ҩ. In the earlier and occasionally in the later period one finds the *rt* ligature: ft. The ligature *st* is regularly used throughout all periods: ft. A *ct* ligature, with a tall broken *c*, is not rare and sometimes resembles *st*. The tendency of *ct* and *rt* to be confused with *st* no doubt was partly responsible for their ultimate disappearance. But a *ct* ligature was developed out of a small *c* which was not open to confusion with *st*: ct. The old ligature for *nt* (N̄) found in capital script continues in use. We find too the ligature *or*, in which the second stroke of the *o* serves also as the first stroke of a capital *r*. The rest of the *r*

[112]

looks like a figure 2 and eventually was used as an independent sign for *r*. Other ligatures are less frequent: *ra, re, ri, rs, ti, us*, etc.

See Plate XII, *b*. Rome, Vat. Urb. lat. 1146, f. 8r. Tours, ninth century. Apicius, I. 21. The "perfected" style of Tours. Note that in the last line not even the *st* of *ligustici* is in ligature.

One of the outstanding characteristics of the Carolingian writing, especially at Tours, was the careful distinction of different styles for different purposes: square capitals, rustic capitals, uncials, half-uncials, and Carolingian minuscule. Square capitals were used for book headings, rustic capitals for explicits, uncials for chapter headings, tables of contents, and first lines, half-uncials for second lines, prefaces, and the like. Thus there was established what has been called the hierarchy of scripts. We are reminded of the superimposition of columns on ancient Roman buildings: Doric, Ionic, Corinthian. Furthermore the older models were followed for the earlier types of script, so that Caroline square capitals look like those of ancient inscriptions and early manuscripts, uncials and half-uncials resemble those found in sixth-century manuscripts. It was almost in-

evitable that as a result of the interest in copying early manuscripts their legibility and beauty
should attract attention and excite emulation.
The process was essentially the same as that
which led to the purification of minuscule under
the influence of half-uncial, though the latter
was preserved as a distinct type. Before the
Carolingian period capitals and uncials were
mixed, took queer forms, and were tricked out
with decorative strokes of all sorts. Sometimes
the Carolingian capitals are so good that they
deceive scholars. Thus a manuscript of Germanicus' *Aratea* at Leiden (Voss. lat. quart.
79) which was written in beautiful rustic capitals in the ninth century has at times been attributed to the fourth century.

See Plate XII, *c.* Leiden, Voss. lat. quart. 79, f.
4r. Ninth century. Germanicus, *Arat.* 23-26.

Many more manuscripts were written in the
ninth century than was formerly supposed. It
used to be common practice to attribute to the
tenth and eleventh centuries manuscripts which
can now be assigned to the ninth. The revision
of the Vulgate by Alcuin led to greater activity
in the copying of manuscripts of the Bible; the
new interest in the classical Latin literature

[114]

caused a larger number of ancient manuscripts to be copied and recopied. In this way the new Carolingian script spread rapidly through France, Germany, and Northern Italy. But always it was affected by local conditions. Thus in some centers, especially in Germany, it was mixed with the local form of Continental Insular.

It should be remembered that the greater number of our classical Latin authors are known to us only in manuscripts written in Carolingian or later script. If we had to depend on manuscripts written before the ninth century for the texts of our classical authors our knowledge of Latin literature would be meager indeed. To put it another way, the ninth-century Renaissance, like every other Renaissance, big or little, was responsible for preserving a number of ancient works that might have disappeared.

We have important manuscripts written in Carolingian script (ninth to twelfth century) of Plautus, Terence, Lucretius, Caesar, Cicero, Sallust, Horace, Ovid, Livy, Persius, Lucan, Seneca, the two Plinys, Quintilian, Statius, Martial, Tacitus, Suetonius, Juvenal, Apuleius, to mention only outstanding names.

Manuscripts written in this script can be, or rather, have been dispensed with only in the case of Virgil because of the existence of manuscripts in capital letters.

We may now summarize the chronological distinctions which have been indicated or implied in the foregoing. Ninth-century characteristics are a preponderance of open *a*'s, especially of the *cc* form; early ligatures, such as *rt* but especially *re*, etc.; open *g;* frequent use of the capital N of half-uncial; well-clubbed tall letters. The tenth century is marked by a great decrease in the number of open *a*'s and the older ligatures except *ct, et, st;* the disappearance of open *g*, first through the closing of the upper loop; the frequency of the tailed *e* (*ę*) for *ae;* the appearance of forms of *i, m, n* with finishing strokes to the right. The eleventh century is distinguished by few outstanding characteristics; it is decidedly a period of transition. Uncial *d* becomes more common; the tick on the *i* is so pronounced that *ui* and *iu* are hard to distinguish; ticks are more frequently found at the tops of tall letters. The twelfth century marks the beginning of Gothic script though some manuscripts are still thoroughly Carolingian. Particularly noteworthy are the huge codices in clear, large letters. Thus the Carolingian hand lasted through the Carolingian and feudal periods. That it survived in the age of feudalism with its separatist tendencies is but a sign of its deep penetration.

See Plate XIII, *a.* London, Brit. Mus. Eg. 818, f. 15r. Eleventh or twelfth century. Solinus, 7. 6-8: *In Laconica spiraculum est Teneron promuntorium adversum Africae in quo fanum Methinnei Arionis quem delfine eo advectum imago testis est aerea ad effigiem casus et veri operis expressa. Preterea tempus signum. Olympiade enim undetricesima qua in certamine Siculo idem Arion victor scribitur, id ipsum gestum probatur. Est et opidum Tenaron nobili vetustate. Preterea aliquot urbes, inter quas Leustrae non obscurae, iam pridem Lacedemoniorum foedo exitu, Amiclae silentio suo quodam pessundatae. Sparta insignis cum Pollucis et Castoris templo, tum etiam Othriadis illustris viri tytulis Theramnae unde primum cultus Dianae Pythane quam Archesilaus stoicus inde ortus pru.* In line 2, *i* is erased before *ariones*, and in line 7 the scribe started to write *Preta* but corrected himself. The mistake *Leustrae* for *Leuctrae* in the same line is due to a *ct* ligature which looked like *st.* *b.* Rome, Vat. lat. 1580, f. 12v. Twelfth century. Virgil, *Georg.* I. 1-7. In line 6 this manuscript has *qui* for the usual *quae.* *c.* Rome, Vat. lat. 9991, f. 19r. Twelfth century. Sallust, *Iug.* I. 1-4.

X. THE GOTHIC SCRIPT OF
THE LATE MIDDLE AGES

VERILY one could read the history of Latin culture as in a mirror in the history of palaeography." [22] We have seen various manifestations of this truism in preceding chapters. We may begin this chapter by tracing the kinship of writing to architecture in connection with one particular style in which it is particularly evident.[23]

Paradoxically, the name " Gothic " for the writing of the thirteenth and following centuries is both a good one and a bad one. It is good in that it suggests Gothic architecture, it is bad in that neither it nor Gothic architecture has anything to do with the Goths. The name was first applied in contempt, as a synonym for " barbarous," by the scholars and critics of the Renaissance.

To give point to the parallelism of Gothic architecture and script, let us go back to the styles just preceding each. Romanesque architecture parallels Carolingian writing in a gen-

eral way. Both are characterized by roundness
and solidity. Both grow out of the late Roman and flourish about the same time in the
same regions — France, Northern Italy, Germany, England. In the case of both there is
even the same dispute whether they originated
in Northern Italy or in France. Be that as it
may, France is the most important center of
both.

Gothic architecture developed gradually out
of Romanesque just as Gothic script grew out
of Carolingian. The period of transition from
the earlier to the later is the twelfth century for
the new architecture as for the new script. The
period of perfection for both is the thirteenth
century, and the country in which they are the
most prominent is France. It has been said
that the French term for the pointed arch of
Gothic, *brisé* ("broken") is more expressive
than the English. "Broken" is a good descrip-
tive term for Gothic script, as mediaeval scholars well realized when they called it *fractura,* a
name which persists to this day in the modern
German appellation *Fraktur* for the Gothic
script still used in Germany.

If Gothic architecture is the great architec-
tural achievement of the Middle Ages and Ro-

manesque is merely an interesting development of Roman style, the same might be said in regard to the script. It is usually held that Carolingian writing spells the greatest advance in mediaeval writing. The parallel of architecture as well as the study of the script itself shows that Carolingian, important as it is historically, is but an outgrowth of Roman writing. The real achievement of the Middle Ages is Gothic script quite as much as Gothic architecture. To be sure, we have said that Gothic developed out of Carolingian, as the latter out of Roman cursive and half-uncial, but Gothic contains more novel elements by far. It lacks clearness, as its companion in the building art sometimes lacks light, and is in general no more adapted to modern conditions than pointed arches, flying buttresses, and mullions, except where a fine appearance only is needed. The beauty of Gothic script at its best is not always appreciated as much as it might be. Those who must read it become as impatient as those who have to live or work in Gothic edifices which have rooms of awkward shape and poor lighting.

It may be argued that the comparison between Gothic script and architecture is superficial, and that it is suggested merely by the chance identity of name. But it should be remembered that writing is an art, a subdivision of painting, with which it was identical at the very beginning, and that all arts are subject to the same tendencies. Like other arts, it has periods when it is highly practical (legible and easily made), and others when it swings away from the utilitarian and almost gives the impression of being practised for its own sake alone.

Gothic architecture was given an impetus by the religious enthusiasm of the twelfth century. Gothic writing was developed in part by the same influence, in part by the twelfth-century Renaissance, which caused the copying of many manuscripts, particularly of the classics. Associated factors are the rise of the universities, especially Paris with its scholasticism and Bologna with its legal studies, and of paid scribes in place of monks. The emergence of the vernacular literature not only led to more copying of books but favored a less formal script. If the tendency towards this style had existed at some other time, it might not have spread because of a lack of intellectual interest and the consequent failure to copy manuscripts in great numbers or because other types were meeting with greater favor.

As a matter of fact, what may be called the Gothic tendency in script has manifested itself at various periods. There is a certain angularity about the pointed Insular hand. More noticeable is the broken appearance of Beneventan, so much so that it has been maintained that it was responsible for the rise of Gothic.[24] But this suggestion is without foundation. Only superficially do the two scripts resemble each other. The methods by which the broken effect is produced are radically different in these two styles of writing. Another kind of writing which has qualities resembling Gothic is Merovingian, and the influence of this in the creation of Gothic is more likely. Merovingian traces continued to be prominent in documents for several centuries after the Carolingian style had become the book hand of Western Europe. That the more cursive style of documents should have an influence on the book hand is not surprising, in view of what happened at earlier periods in the history of Roman script. But let us see what the characteristics of Gothic are.

The angularity of Gothic has already been mentioned. The neatly rounded Carolingian characters are not easy to make. A scribe who is in a hurry tends to make a round shaded letter in a series of short strokes. Thus a circle becomes a polygon. Beyond a certain point, however, angularity is no more rapid than perfect roundness, and the time came when exaggerated angularity was preferred for its own sake.

Again, Gothic is more crowded laterally. The saving of space as well as of time is important. Here the Merovingian parallel is most instructive. Especially in the first lines of Merovingian documents one finds a peculiarly crowded effect — a picket fence style. This persists even in the documents written in Carolingian letters in the twelfth century.

See Plate XIV, *a*. London, Brit. Mus. Harl. lat. 2655, f. 1r. Twelfth or thirteenth century. Ovid, *Fast.* 22–38. In line 27 *Romulus* is written above; in the margin: *Nota decem anni menses et eorum nomina*, both by a fourteenth-century hand. In line 32 *teneatur* was corrected to *tueatur* and the next word *amor* was deleted.

Associated with compression and angularity in the desire to save space and time is the use of abbreviations. These increase enormously in Gothic, both through independent development and in part through the influence of Insular manuscripts.

Compression was also responsible for a characteristic of Gothic which is more important and novel than any other, although at first glance it is not so noticeable as other features. This is a combination of letters in a fashion which is not commonly found in earlier scripts. It is not the type that we call ligature, nor is it the " union " or touching of letters which we find in Beneventan. It is rather an outgrowth of the latter method, though that does not mean that it is due to Beneventan influence. Unions are found sporadically in various scripts. But the Gothic goes beyond unions, which are mere contacts of letters even if these contacts are harmonious. In Gothic there is genuine fusion, in which two letters have a member in common, like Siamese twins. In the so-called unions there is only adhesion; in the fusions, cohesion. Of course certain kinds of ligatures, especially the old ones, such as ℕ for *nt,* are based on this general principle, but the new type of fusion is not derived from such ligatures. It consists of the running together of two rounds letters. The round portions must touch; thus we may have *o, b, p,* uncial *d,* followed by *c, e, g, o, q,* but not *o* followed by *b,* or *c* followed by *o,* etc. Occasionally the usage is extended, *e.g.* to *bb, pp,* etc.; this last in fact occurs early. In such fusions the stroke in common was written twice, in contrast to the *nt* and similar ligatures. Thus the *o* of *bo* is not a mere appendage of the *b.* It is this characteristic that is probably referred to by a fourteenth-century chronicle in using the term *textura* (in conjunction with *fractura*) of the current script. The letters are truly woven together.

See Plate XIV, *b.* Rome, Vat. lat. 702, f. 295v. Thirteenth century. Alexander de Hales, *Summa* II, end. The more difficult abbreviations are: *vel, quantum, que, sunt et, ambulavit, veritatem, hoc est quantum, et secundum hoc non, modo ipsum, aliud est quam materiam peccati, nec, simile, quando Thimoceum circumcidit, tentris, hoc enim fecit, quod, poneret, cerimonialia, gencium.* Note the English *w* in *ewangelii.* At the end is a fourteenth-century note of which all is erased except the first two words, *Iste liber.* In the erasure a fifteenth-century hand wrote: *est mei Thome de Sarzana qui servio Domino Episcopo Bononiensi.* This Thomas later became Pope Nicholas V.

[125]

Still another general characteristic of Gothic is the heavy shading. The desire for decoration, characteristic of Gothic art, leads to a great development of hair lines, hooks, and similar embellishments.

In the matter of letter forms Gothic continues certain Carolingian tendencies. The *a* is uncial but takes on various shapes. Sometimes the top curves well over and joins the lower closed part of the letter. Again the top all but disappears. Or it is greatly prolonged before curving to the left and causes the letter to resemble a minuscule *d*. The *c* sometimes cannot be distinguished from *t;* at other times it closely resembles *e,* which often has a mere hook instead of a loop. The uncial *d* (ƀ) becomes more and more frequent. In some manuscripts both uncial and minuscule forms are used together without distinction. In others, one alone is found. In still others distinctions are made between the two, such as giving preference to the uncial form at the end of a word or line or before a round letter, so that fusion may take place.

When two *i*'s were used together, faint slanting lines were placed above them to distinguish from *u*. Since a number of letter combinations became unclear as a result of the angular style, *i* strokes began to be used over single *i*'s as well, especially when used in combination with *m, n, u*. The first of these practices began in the eleventh or twelfth century but did not become regular until the thirteenth; the second followed it by about a generation. The descendants of these lines are our dots, which first made their appearance in the fourteenth century. The use of *ij* to distinguish double *i* from *u* also began about the twelfth century.

The round 2-shaped *r*, used after *o* and derived from an ancient ligature of *or*, was inherited by Gothic from Carolingian. Like the uncial *d*, it became more common in the Gothic period. Although restricted for a long time to the combination with *o*, it really was regarded as a separate letter. As early as the tenth century sporadic examples of this round *r* occur after other round letters besides *o*. By the beginning of the thirteenth century this became a regular practice. Another system, less common, to be sure, which seems to have begun in the fourteenth century, was to use round *r* after all the vowels, not merely *o*. Eventually the ordinary *r* all but disappears in fifteenth-century Italian Gothic. An occasional Carolingian custom of using *or* before vowels and o2 before consonants became more frequent in the Gothic period. Being extended to *ar*, etc., it came to mean that 2 was used only before consonants. In the end there was much confusion.

In the twelfth century round *s* (similar to our present letter) becomes more and more common at the end of a word; later it is used occasionally in other parts of the word. The curves generally are closed, giving the letter the appearance of a figure 8. At the beginning of a word *u* is often written *v*, but no distinction is made between vowel and consonant. In fifteenth-century German Gothic a hook is put over *u* to distinguish from *n*, a practice which persists in modern German cursive Gothic.

See Plate XIV, *c.* Rome, Vat. lat. 833, f. 27r. Fourteenth century. Aegidius, *Comm. in Arist. Rhet.* I. 11. A fine example of scholastic abbreviation. The more difficult signs are to be expanded thus: *Deinde cum dicit, delectabile postquam ostendit quod speciales, expectationes, venatur, considerationes, per comparationem, et duo facit secundum, sensitivus, videtur, dividit, scilicet, concupiscibilem primo ergo, huiusmodi, respectu irascibilis secundo, vindictam, honorem, ideo ostendit, esse.*

Of the old ligatures only *st* is commonly preserved; the *ct* and *et* ligatures are much rarer.

The *ae* ligature is rare, as *ae* is usually written *e*.

There are great differences in the Gothic of different periods and places. In Northern France, where Gothic began, progress is rapid; in more remote regions the script may look older than it is. The beginnings of the Gothic tendencies are discernible in the eleventh century, but the period of incubation is really the twelfth. In the thirteenth the script is at its best in France. A tiny script which is beautiful but hard to read becomes popular in pocket editions of the Bible and other books. These are in striking contrast to some of the very large books of the preceding century, when an unusually large script was cultivated. The hesitation between round and square which gives an appearance of awkwardness to much twelfth-century writing, disappears in the thirteenth, and rigid perfection grows out of a new confidence.

In the meantime a new cursive script on the Gothic model came into being. This in turn modified the book hand, all the more so because the cheapening of the writing material by the substitution of paper for parchment led to the more general and less careful copying of books. The most noticeable effect of cursive is in flourishes attached to long letters. At first there is mere bending of the long strokes; then comes a short hair line; finally a long finishing stroke that often bends back towards the line of writing and produces loops. When these flourishes are hair lines carefully distinguished from the main strokes, the appearance is not necessarily bad, but heavy flourishes tend to make an overloaded script. In the cursive and semi-cursive scripts complete angularity yields in part to rounding. Very often the result is a very ugly and illegible script.

First evidences of these influences are to be seen in the thirteenth century, *e.g.* in the *littera Parisiensis,* but the developed form is the *littera bastarda,* a mixed cursive and book script of the fourteenth and fifteenth centuries. The flourishes run down to the right from the tops of the tall letters. Especially in the French *bastarda,* an unlovely script, the main strokes of the letters which extend below the line thin out somewhat as in pointed Insular. This is particularly noticeable in the long *s,* which extends above and below the line and swells in the middle. In the most characteristic examples of this script the *s* dominates the page. In its later form this script develops a slope.

Alongside the more cursive *bastarda* the older, more formal script continued in use under the name *textura*. In the fifteenth century we sometimes find both used in the same manuscript, *e.g.* the *textura* for Latin, the *bastarda* for German. In general the *bastarda* is more commonly used for the vernacular. Cursive script and vernacular speech naturally go together.

In Italy the history of Gothic script, like that of Gothic architecture, was quite different from what it was north of the Alps in France, Germany, the Netherlands, and England. The writing did not go nearly as far in developing compression, broken lines, and angularity; it is a decidedly round script, relatively speaking, and goes under the name of *rotunda*. In other respects it is thoroughly Gothic, *e.g.* in its fusions, in the multiplicity of its abbreviations, and in its heavy shading. One variety is the *littera Bononiensis*, perfected in the copying of juristic manuscripts at Bologna, famous for the legal instruction at its university. A less formal type of rotunda, smaller, less shaded, and

rounder, is almost humanistic in style. Such
was the formal writing of Petrarch, for example. A cursive Gothic too, with flourishes,
arose in Italy. Petrarch used this in less formal writing; sometimes he (like others) mixed
the two.

See Plate XV, *a*. Paris, Bibl. Nat. lat. 1994, f.
1r. Italian cursive (*bastarda*), dated 1337. Autograph of Petrarch. Note that the addition in line 3
is not in cursive but in the *rotunda* which Petrarch
generally used in books: *Considerare debemus assi-
due peccata que fecimus et vitam nostram Aut excusa-
tionem criminum captantes sed corde et ore sim gentes
sed nudantes et medici celestis auxilium implorantes.
Inque erubescere et iram iusti iudicis et iudicii diem
et hoc primo. Non tamen usque adeo ut umquam de
immensa dei m altero erratum fuerit. Siquidem in
primo hec tria m semper odiosa est deinde peccatorum
veterum licentior consue desperatio primum malorum
omnium extremum. Tum et que.*

At its best Gothic is beautiful but hard to
read; at its worst it is extremely ugly and illegible. In the various types letter confusions
of various sorts developed. Most notable was
the confusion brought about by the angularity
of *i, u, m, n*. Strokes and dots for *i*, hooks for
u helped to remedy this defect. How well this

weakness was realized is indicated by an anecdote composed in the thirteenth or fourteenth century for the purpose of illustrating the difficulties of the script. The story tells of a letter sent to the senate at Rome by actors of small stature expressing their unwillingness to give up their function of distributing to the actors the wine obtained from certain vineyards near the walls: [25]

mimi numinum niuium minimi munium nimium uini muniminum imminui uiui minimum uolunt.

"The very short mimes of the gods of snow do not at all wish that during their lifetime the very great burden [munium *is neuter singular*] of (distributing) the wine of the walls to be lightened." When this is written in Gothic characters without dots for the *i*'s and with *v* written as *u*, it makes a first-class riddle.

There are many classical manuscripts in Gothic script, but, curiously enough, only in rare instances are they our oldest manuscripts of the ancient authors. We have available either Carolingian manuscripts or else none before the humanistic period. Thus all the works of the prolific Ovid, the favorite of the thirteenth century, are known to us in copies of the ninth to twelfth centuries, though the number of thirteenth-century manuscripts of his works is very large. It is true that the one extant eleventh-century copy of the *Tristia* is incomplete, but there was another copy of the same age which disappeared in the fifteenth century. The oldest manuscript of Cornelius Nepos was written in the twelfth or thirteenth century in an incipient Gothic which can hardly be called a good example of that script. The earliest copy of Cicero's letters to Atticus (Florence, Laur. 49.18) is in a fourteenth-century cursive hand, an Italian *bastarda*. The three oldest manuscripts of Catullus (at Oxford, Paris, Rome) are in Italian *rotunda* of the fourteenth century, though the latter two, especially the Paris manuscript, begin to show cursive and humanistic traits. The oldest manuscript of Tibullus, in the Ambrosian library at Milan, is another example of modified *rotunda*. But these manuscripts of Cicero, Catullus, and Tibullus owe their copying to the new humanism of such men as Petrarch and Coluccio Salutati. The significance of these facts is that between the Carolingian period and the Italian Renaissance there was no real revival of classical interest, at least none comparable with these two periods.

We may now summarize and add to the criteria for dating Gothic manuscripts. The twelfth century is marked by the appearance of the characteristic Gothic features in incipient form (angularity, compression, fusion), of strokes over *ii*, and of a long-tailed *h*, by the greater frequency of round *d* and *s*, the latter especially at the end of a word, by the disappearance of the ligature *ae*, which caused the diphthong to be writteen as *e*, and by the substitution of *c* for *t* before *i* plus vowel (as in *oracio* for *oratio*). In the thirteenth century the Gothic qualities are fully developed and easily recognized; the script is clearly angular but in a natural rather than an artificial way. Fusions are more numerous. The stroke is now used over single as well as double *i; n* and *u* become more and more alike; *c* and *t* are often indistinguishable; round *s* is often found in the interior of a word as well as the end; round *d* becomes the more usual form, *v* comes to be used at the beginning of a word (for vowel or consonant) while *u* is retained elsewhere. The old *ct* ligature is now commonly written in two parts, the connecting stroke being attached to the *t*. In the fourteenth century the cursive hand with its flourishes attracts attention. In the formal script the uncial *a* with top turned back to make a two-looped letter is the regular form; dots instead of strokes begin to appear over the *i*'s; round *s* (in the closed form) and *d* are dominant. In the fifteenth century cursive and semi-cursive hands which are hard to read are numerous. Abbreviations attain their maximum growth. The older, more formal script becomes artificial.

XI. THE WRITING OF THE ITALIAN RENAISSANCE

IN THE fourteenth century there began in Italy that movement in the history of civilization which we call the Italian Renaissance. Among the many characteristics of this movement one of the chief was the interest in classical Latin literature as distinguished from mediaeval, and another was a freshness of outlook and a willingness to depart from tradition. As a result of the first characteristic the humanists of the fourteenth and fifteenth centuries had occasion to examine numerous early manuscripts of classical authors which had lain unused and forgotten in the libraries of Western Europe. Among these manuscripts there were many of the ninth and tenth centuries, written during that earlier Renaissance when the Carolingian handwriting was produced as a reform of the preceding script. Because of this greater familiarity with the excellent handwriting which preceded the Gothic and of the willingness to break with tradition, the Italian

[137]

humanists began to simplify their Gothic script which to be sure had never been as intricate as that north of the Alps. Thus the new writing was not a reaction against extreme Gothic forms, as is sometimes stated, but rather a gradual simplification of a relatively plain Gothic, under Carolingian influence.

This simplified Gothic was, as we have seen, used by Petrarch, commonly called the first of the humanists. That he did so is no accident, for we know from his own remarks that he objected to the intricate form of Gothic, saying that it was attractive to look at but hard to read, produced by artists rather than scribes, and that he aimed at a clear script.[26]

Coluccio Salutati, the famous founder of humanism at Florence, is sometimes cited as an initiator of humanistic script because in a letter written in 1395 he expressed preference for a manuscript copied in *antiqua littera*. This has been interpreted in accordance with the later use of *antiqua* (still current) as referring to the imitation of Carolingian script, which the humanists mistook for that of antiquity. But Coluccio's letter is addressed to Jean de Montreuil of France, where, as Coluccio must have known, humanistic script was not cultivated.

[138]

Coluccio probably meant a copy going back to the twelfth century, when the book which he wanted (the letters of Abélard) was composed.[27] Coluccio's own writing is a simplified Gothic like Petrarch's, with regular use of uncial *d* and frequent use of fusions and round *r*. Whether he is also responsible for writing in which there was an admixture of humanistic elements, such as the straight *d*, as has at times been maintained, is still uncertain. It is certain, however, that he sometimes avoided fusions.

See Plate XV, *b*. London, Brit. Mus. Add. 11987, f. 175v. Late fourteenth century, hand of the Florentine humanist Coluccio Salutati. Seneca, *Herc. Oet.*, end.

At any rate, it was at the turn of the century that the direct imitation of Carolingian began. In the hands of some this was only partial, and such partial imitation continued for a long time. Fusions became less numerous or disappeared entirely. Letters became simpler, though not always rounder. Shading decreased. Thus writing went through the same stages as the revival of learning with which it was associated: a partial reawakening with many mediaeval survivals in the fourteenth century and the

[139]

full-blown Renaissance in the fifteenth. The Renaissance did not "come up like thunder." But even in the fifteenth century there was much Gothic writing and much mediaeval culture still left, and the revival of earlier script and culture took many different forms.

A more or less complete humanistic script appears at Florence in the early part of the fifteenth century. The first dated examples are from the hand of Poggio, the well-known humanist and disciple of Coluccio Salutati. The oldest manuscript known to have been written by him in the new hand is dated 1408, a copy of Cicero's letters to Atticus (Berlin, Ham. 166).[28] From December of the same year or January of the next we have the copy he made of Eusebius (Florence, Laur. 67.15). It is interesting to note that in the former uncial *a* is used, in the latter the minuscule form of some Gothic styles. There are occasional fusions and " unions." The general style is that of the eleventh century; *e.g.* round *s* is avoided. Of course Poggio also used a Gothic script for less formal use as well as a mixture of the two.

See Plate XV, *c.* Florence, Laur. 48, 22, f. 9r. Written by the humanist Poggio, probably in 1425. Cicero, *Phil.* II. 10.

There was much variation in the humanistic script, according as earlier or later Carolingian models were followed. In general it resembles Carolingian of the tenth and eleventh centuries rather than that of the ninth or twelfth. The tall letters do not have the graceful clubbing of the ninth century, there are no open *a*'s and no ligatures except those which continued in use throughout the Carolingian period. On the other hand, the twelfth-century premonitions of Gothic are absent, such as angularity and the greater frequency of uncial *d* and round *r*.

See Plate XVI, *a*. Rome, Vat. Ott. lat. 1202, f. 14v. Dated Florence, 1426. Tibullus, I. 6. 66–72. There are several corrections in these lines; thus in the sixth line *peccasse* was written by a different hand, partly in erasure. In the last line, all except the first two letters was added by a different hand, probably that of the well-known humanist, Giovanni Aurispa.

Occasionally scripts other than Carolingian served in part as models. Thus the well-known humanist Pontanus sometimes imitated Beneventan, especially in the letter *e*, in his Tacitus (Leiden, Periz. 18. Q. 21) and his Tibullus (Wolfenbüttel, Aug. 82.6 fol.), written about 1460. For capitals not only the Carolingian script but also the ancient inscriptions served as models.

Even when the writing follows a Carolingian model closely it is not really difficult to distinguish the two. The humanistic uncial *a* often has a top carried well to the left, as in Gothic, much more so than in Carolingian. The *i* may have a dot or stroke, as in Gothic; double *i* is differentiated from *u* by dots or strokes or by the form *ij*. The vertical stroke of the *t* extends above the cross stroke, as in late Gothic. There may be finishing strokes turning to the right at the base of the script. There is variation of practice in regard to *s*. At first the long *s* of earlier writing dominates; at times only the round *s* is used; eventually the Gothic usage (round *s* at the end of a word and the long *s* elsewhere) triumphs. Ligatures are confined as a rule to *ae, ct, et,* and *st*. Abbreviations are less numerous than in Gothic manuscripts, but some are very common, such as the signs for *que, quae, qui, quam, quod, per, prae, pro, m, n.*

See Plate XVI, *b*. Chicago, University of Chicago. Dated 1481. Barozzi, *Carmina, Praef.* The abbreviations stand for *preter (praeter), quoque, internitionem, Romam, unquam, fluxus, periculosissimas.*

Note that in spite of the carefulness of the script there is no complete regularity in the use of the round and long *s*. The latter is always used at the end of a word and the former, when single, in the interior, but *ss*, while usually written with two long *s*'s, may also be expressed by round *s* followed by long *s*.

A cursive form of the new script sprang up rapidly, and formal scripts with cursive elements also appeared early. Connecting strokes are exaggerated. Hooks appear at the tops and bottoms of long letters. Long strokes tend to bend. Shading disappears entirely, and uniformly thin strokes are found in books for the first time since papyrus times. Letters take exaggerated forms: *g* may have a large lower loop, in various shapes; long *s* not only extends below the line but also has a long sweeping curve at the top. Gothic characteristics maintain themselves in part, such as uncial *d*, the round *a* of Gothic cursive, round *r*, often with an initial connecting stroke. The writing tends to develop a slope. Eventually two main hands arose, the formal hand which is the ancestor of our roman type fonts and the sloping cursive which became the model for our italics. We make a sharp differentiation between these

[143]

types, but we should not forget that in the fifteenth century there were many intermediate forms, such as vertical writing with cursive elements in greater or less degree, sloping writing with formal elements, semi-sloping styles. Much more copying of books was done by educated men who were not professional scribes, and the natural tendency was to develop a simple, rapid script.

See Plate XVI, *c.* Leiden, Voss. lat. oct. 76, f. 56r. Dated 1451. Tibullus, I. 1. 56–63.

Classical works known in whole or part only through fifteenth-century manuscripts chiefly in humanistic or semi-humanistic script are Asconius (*e.g.* Poggio's copy at Madrid, 10.81), some of Cicero's speeches and some of his rhetorical works, Petronius' *Cena* in Paris 7989, written in 1423 in an angular semi-humanistic script, the *Panegyrici* (including Pliny's speech), Silius Italicus, Statius' *Silvae*, Suetonius' *De grammaticis et rhetoribus*, Tacitus' *Dialogus, Agricola,* and *Germania.*

XII. THE INVENTION OF PRINT-
ING AND THE MODERN PERIOD

I F WE take the word " printing " in its literal
sense of pressing or stamping, the invention was a very early one, illustrated by ancient seals, Roman brick stamps, etc. But in
regard to the alphabet we mean by printing the
use of movable type, for that was the invention which made reproduction of books rapid.
The question has sometimes been asked why
the practical Romans did not invent printing.
Apart from the answer that they simply did
not, just as they did not invent other things
familiar to us, it may be said that the conditions were not favorable: labor for copying
manuscripts was relatively cheap, the demand
for books was less great, suitable printing materials such as paper and printer's ink were unknown. As Carter has said: [29] " While it was
the coming of paper that made the invention of
printing possible, it was the invention of printing that made the use of paper general."

Block printing (*i.e.* where the entire page,

not the individual character, was cut in a block of wood) began in China at least as early as the eighth century. Printing from movable type was invented there in the eleventh century but never became general because the Chinese language is written with too many characters. Block printing seems to have begun in Europe at the end of the fourteenth century. Playing cards (originally introduced from China) were first made in Europe by block printing not later than the beginning of the fifteenth century. The presumption is that the method of printing was imported from the East as well as the use of playing cards. But that printing from movable types was introduced into Europe from China is not substantiated by any real evidence. Indications are that it was independently invented in Europe.

Who the inventor of printing was is still veiled in mystery. The most generally accepted view is that he was Johann Gutenberg of Mainz. He did not print his name on any of the books attributed to him, but his first dated work, a papal indulgence, was issued in 1454, though some think that we have earlier specimens of his work. The famous 42-line Bible, his first certain book, was published not

later than 1456.[30] The first book with a date
and printer's name on it was a psalter issued

BIBLE, MAINZ, 1456, GUTENBERG

by Johann Fust and Peter Schoeffer, the successors of Gutenberg, in 1457.

From Mainz the new invention spread to
other German cities, and from Germany to

CICERO, EPIST. AD FAM., ROME, 1467, SWEYNHEYM
AND PANNARTZ

other countries. At first all the printers were
German. In Italy the first book was printed
in 1464 in the monastery at Subiaco by Conrad
Sweynheym and Arnold Pannartz, who are

thought to have learned the new art in the shop
of Fust and Schoeffer.[31]   The book was a
" Donatus," or Latin grammar.   Their second
book was Cicero's *De oratore*.   In 1467 they
moved to Rome.   The art grew rapidly in
Italy, especially in Venice.   Before 1500 there
were 268 printers in that city, 63 in Milan, and
41 in Rome.   Among the most famous Venetian printers were Johann of Speyer (Spiren-
sis), who printed the first book at Venice in
1469 (Cicero's *Letters*), his brother Wendelin,
Nicolas Jenson, famous for his type fonts, and
Aldus Manutius, first printer of small books, of

E   t Vindelino debebis tu quoq: formis
Egregie impreffit has modo qui decadas:
A   tq ipfas iifdem fcpuis uelut hoftibus acri
Bello oppugnatas fortiter eripuit.

LIVY, VENICE, 1470, JENSON

italic type (1501), and (unfortunately) of cursive Greek fonts (1495).   The first Greek book
was printed at Milan in 1476 in a much clearer
type.

In France the first book was printed in
1470.   It is interesting to note that Guillaume
Fichet, one of the men responsible for bringing

German printers to France, fully realized the importance of the new art. He pointed out that Bacchus and Ceres were deified because they taught man the use of wine and bread, but that Gutenberg's invention was even more divine since it enabled man to preserve for posterity all that is said or thought.

In England the first printing was done by William Caxton in 1476 and his first book was issued in 1477. He learned and practised the trade on the Continent before he set up his shop in his native land. He was the first non-German printer to introduce the art into a new country. Also, his first printing was in English, not Latin as elsewhere. In the Americas the first book was printed in Mexico City in 1539. The imprint credits it to a printer of German origin, Juan Cromberger, who plied his trade in Spain. Yet Cromberger never crossed the Atlantic but sent an Italian over. Printing was truly international in those days! In the English Colonies which afterwards became the United States the first press was established in Cambridge, Mass., in 1638, but the first published book of which we know dates from 1640.

As has been said, the really important invention in connection with the printing of alphabetic writing was that of movable type. Yet, curiously enough, recent printing inventions — linotyping and plate printing — seem like a step backward to block printing. In the former the actual printing is done from a solid line of type, in the latter, from solid pages. Of course the principle of movable type has not been abandoned in these processes.

The early printers based their fonts on the writing which was current in books of their day. They imitated it as closely as possible so that their product might not suffer by comparison. Thus the early German books were printed in the Gothic letters then favored in Germany, though in a rather plain Gothic. The first books printed at Subiaco were in a simplified Gothic, but this did not find favor with the Italians who had accepted the Renaissance script. So when Sweynheym and Pannartz moved to Rome they began to use what we have called " roman " type ever since — a font based on the book hand of Italy. This soon became the regular Italian type, though the Italian Gothic (*rotunda*) was widely used for a time, especially in Venice. In other countries too the German or German-trained printers introduced the Gothic types (especially *rotunda*), but in these countries it was less quickly abandoned. In Spain there were chiefly the *rotunda* and the *textura* (the native formal Gothic). Caxton used *textura* and *bastarda* — the latter (a cursive Gothic) more often for books in English. German printers used roman or modified roman occasionally almost from the beginning (the first example is from Strasbourg, 1464) but preferred the *rotunda*, alongside the native *textura*. The latter was used especially for Bibles and religious works. Gradually *rotunda* came to be regarded in Germany as the appropriate type for Latin, and various kinds of *bastarda* came to be used for the vernacular, as in England and also France. Out of these there developed a more elaborate style, called *fractura*, in the early fifteenth century, in the development of which Dürer played a part. This has remained the basic German type. The *rotunda* was early abandoned for roman in the printing of Latin.

As already stated, Aldus Manutius first used what we call " italic " type in April 1501 (Virgil). He simply adopted the cursive slanting form of humanistic writing. The absurd statement is still commonly made that Aldus based this font on the handwriting of Petrarch. But there is no similarity between the two. Aldus printed whole books in the new font; its restriction to special purposes, such as foreign words and quotations, is more recent.

N *os patriam fugimus;tu Tityre lentus in umbra*
F *ormosam resonare doces Amaryllida syluas.*
·O *Meliboee,deus nobis haec ocia fecit·*   Ti·
N *anq; erit ille mihi semper deus,illius aram*
S *aepe tener nostris ab ouilibus imbuet agnus.*
I *lle meas errare boues,ut cernis,et ipsum*

VIRGIL, VENICE, 1501.   FIRST ITALICS USED
BY ALDUS MANUTIUS

Printing types have varied more or less from the beginning but the best examples of humanistic script have usually been taken as models. The excellence of early printing has been attributed to its faithful imitation of manuscripts. Many fonts are without shading or with weak shading, like some of the humanistic scripts. When there is shading the letters are symmetrical, like those produced by a straight pen in writing; thus the *o* is not tilted, as in the "slanted-pen" style.

The close relation of writing and art was discussed in the chapter on Gothic script. The parallelism could be extended to other periods of writing and applies to printing equally well. The humanistic writing on which type was based was but one expression of Renaissance art. Changes in artistic taste since the fifteenth century have left their impress on our type fonts — now plain and solid, now fragile and elaborate.

In Chapter V we discussed a few of the factors that played a part in the evolution of the alphabet. How varied and unexpected such factors may be is indicated by a thought thrown out by Updike. Reminding us that since the eighteenth century the opening words of Cicero's first speech against Catiline (*Quo usque tandem,* etc.) have commonly been used in type specimens, he points out that type-founders lengthened the tail of the Q in order to outdo each other: " I do not say that Q's have long tails because Cicero delivered an oration against Catiline; but that the tails of some Q's would not be as long as they are if the oration had begun with some other word! " [32]

Printing, making use of the formal and semiformal scripts in use at the time of its invention and early development, became purely formal. At the same time handwriting continued its own way. Its formal use was greatly diminished

since most books were produced by the printing press. So it developed the more cursive
styles, in which words could be written with
little or no lifting of the pen from the paper.
In this way the loops and connecting strokes of
our "script" have developed. In the course
of time there have arisen varieties of cursive
script, some more, some less formal. The relation of script to italic type (for italic type, derived as it is from cursive humanistic writing,
is its closest relative) may be seen by comparing the alphabets:

a b c d e f g h i j k l m n o p q r s t u v w x y z

abcdefghijklmnopqrstuvwxyz

The loops of the long letters are due to the desire to connect with preceding or following letters without lifting the pen; thus the upper loop
of *f* is connected with the preceding, the lower
with the following letter. The shape of *e* is explained when we note that the loop is made first
in order to connect with the preceding letter.
The *r* is sometimes explained as a relic of the
2-shaped *r*, but humanistic examples indicate
that it is the regular *r* made in one stroke. The
s is a round one, but the connecting stroke at the

[154]

beginning caused the upper curve to be eliminated almost entirely. In the old-fashioned long *s* (similar to our *f*) it is the lower curve which has disappeared.

At the present time there is a movement on foot, especially in England, to return to the beautiful humanistic hands and to abandon our common cursive script. Such " manuscript writing " is being taught in many schools.

It remains to discuss our present alphabet as compared with the Roman. In addition to the twenty-three letters of the Roman alphabet we have *j, v,* and *w.* The Romans used *i* and *u* for both vowel and consonant, just as we use *y* with both values (e.g. *by, you*). The original forms were I (what we now call the vowel) and V (our present consonant). Long forms of *i* and round forms of *v* were developed in antiquity but were not differentiated in usage (except that the tall I sometimes represented the lengthened vowel). In the Middle Ages the long *i* remained exceptional (being used only in certain scripts under certain circumstances with no distinction between vowel and consonant). The round *u* became the regular form, and *v* was used only occasionally. The modern distinctions were not made until the

sixteenth century and did not become general
in England until the seventeenth. The capital
forms U and J are especially late. The latter
was previously used as a capital I, as it still is
at times in the Roman script of Germany. In
the King James Bible (1611) *J* and *j* are not
used, nor are they found in the text of the Shakspere Folio of 1623. In dictionaries words beginning with *u* and *v* were combined for a long
time after the distinction was made. Only since
the first edition of Webster (1828) have the
words beginning with *u* been regularly printed
before those whose initial is *v*. The supplement of the " British Museum Catalogue of
Printed Books," issued in 1904, still inter-
mingles words whose initials are *u* and *v*. In the
printer's " upper case " the capital letters are
arranged alphabetically, but J and U still come
after Z, owing to the unwillingness of printers
to re-learn the familiar position of the letters
established before J and U were known. And
that is only right: as new letters (for their
restriction in use makes them new) they should
have taken their places at the end of the line,
but their sisters, I and V, squeezed over and
made room for them, much to the disgust and
indignation, no doubt, of the other letters.

[156]

There remains *w*. As this has the sound of the consonantal *u* of classical Latin it may be asked why *u* was not used for that sound in English. The reason is that Latin consonantal *u* had taken on the sound of modern *v* when Anglo-Saxon first began to be written with the Latin letters and accordingly was adopted for that sound. So in the seventh century Anglo-Saxon began to use two *u*'s, or " double u," for the sound no longer represented in Latin. In the eighth century *w* was superseded by the runic character wen for this sound, but in the meantime *w* had spread to Germany and France. In the eleventh century the Normans brought it back to England. After several centuries of strife it triumphed over the interloper wen. To-day it is looked upon as a characteristic letter of English and German, and Italian printers love to introduce it in quoting an English word, whether it is correctly used or not, as if no English word were complete without it. Yet it merely represents a simple sound found in classical Latin as well as in the Germanic tongues. The English *wine* represents Latin *vinum* more accurately, as far as the sound of the first letter is concerned, than do French *vin* or Italian *vino*. As for its two parents, *u*

[157]

and *v, w* retains the name of the former and the appearance of the latter. For a long time it was written as two letters, *uu* or *vv*. As a result of the addition of *v* and *w* we now have five descendants of the Semitic *vau*, the most prolific letter in the alphabet. They are *f, u, v, w, y.* This large family makes up nearly twenty per cent of the membership of the exclusive society of characters which we call the alphabet.

XIII. THE SPREAD OF THE LATIN ALPHABET

THE HUMANISTIC script permeated Italy first and passed from there to the various countries of Western Europe along with the revival of learning. So it came to France, Spain, and England in the sixteenth century, but in England the old Gothic maintained itself for a long time, especially in books dealing with the law. Thus in the matter of writing as in other respects the law shows its conservative character. In cursive writing too the old Gothic, or " secretary " hand, as it was called, was reluctant to yield place to the new intruder, but by the seventeenth century the " sweet Roman hand," as Shakspere calls it in *Twelfth Night,* had the field to itself. In Holland the Roman was introduced in the sixteenth century and had entirely superseded the Gothic by the nineteenth. The Scandinavian countries, including Finland, gave up Gothic in the nineteenth century and now make exclusive use of the Roman style.

In Germany the humanistic script did not drive out the Gothic, and the latter remains still the dominant style of writing of Germany and Austria. This is due in part to the mistaken feeling that the Gothic is a national script. So strongly was Bismarck impressed with this view that he refused to read books printed in Roman type. Yet Gothic was no more characteristic of Germany than of France, England, and Italy in the thirteenth and fourteenth centuries. As a matter of fact, the Germans would have a better case for claiming Carolingian as a national script than Gothic. But even in Germany the humanistic style, which is now usually referred to as *antiqua*, has made wide inroads and bids fair to drive out the Gothic in the course of time, though it would seem rash to make any positive prediction on this point. Scientific books are regularly printed in Roman in Germany, and this is taught in the schools by the side of Gothic. Newspapers and popular works are printed in the old Gothic type. Of the books published in 1881, 62 per cent were in the Gothic " Fraktur," 38 per cent in Roman.

The form of the Latin alphabet developed in Ireland during the flourishing period of Irish culture in the Middle Ages has never been entirely given up in the writing of Gaelic. But the Roman writing is more common in spite of nationalistic attempts to encourage the " national " hand.

The regions of Western Europe in which Latin was the dominant language in ancient times all use the humanistic script. Through colonization it has spread to North and South America, Africa, Australia, and parts of Asia. Ireland and Germany, which were not part of the Roman Empire, use it together with older forms of the Latin alphabet.

In Eastern Europe the leading language of the Roman Empire was Greek, and to-day the one competitor of the Latin alphabet in that region is the Greek and its most important offshoot, Cyrillic. Even in Greece there is a movement to abandon its historic alphabet in favor of the Latin, as noted in an earlier chapter, but it cannot be said that it has made much progress. At the present time the Cyrillic alphabet is practically synonymous with the Russian, though Bulgaria and in part Jugoslavia also use it. In Russia there has been agitation in the last few years to adopt the Latin alphabet. In view of official encouragement of the plan it seems not unlikely that it will be carried out eventually. The Western Slavic nations, Poland and Czechoslovakia, have employed the Latin alphabet from the beginning as a result of affiliation with the Roman church; in the same way the Roman Catholic portions of Jugoslavia use the Latin letters.

In Rumania, whose speech is a Romance language akin to French, Italian, etc., the Cyrillic alphabet was used for a long time, under Bulgarian influence. It is only since 1860 that the Latin alphabet has had exclusive rights in Rumanian schools and government offices. Hungarian has always been written in the Latin alphabet.

Until recently the Turks made use of the Arabic alphabet in writing their language, and this alphabet is a direct descendent of the ancient Semitic via the Nabataean. But by an act of the Turkish parliament in 1928 it was decreed that this alphabet was to be abandoned in favor of the Latin, and preparations were made for this difficult and revolutionary change. It was argued in behalf of this reform that the Arabic alphabet was too complicated and that nearly a hundred different letter signs had to be learned. The movement in favor of the Roman alphabet began in 1908, but it is the Westernizing tendency of the present government of Turkey which led to its final adoption. The change affects the order of writing as well, now from left to right instead of right to left. The action of Turkey marks an important break in the association of Arabic script with Mohammedanism.

In Western Asia the prevalent alphabet is the Arabic, and there is little chance that this will be given up in the near future if at all. In Palestine the square Hebrew alphabet is also used. This is the script of the Hebrew Bible and other Hebrew books used by Jews throughout the world, as well as of the Yiddish language. This alphabet is descended from the ancient Semitic through the Aramaic. It will no doubt continue to be used by the Jews for cultural and nationalistic purposes. The many alphabets of Central Asia (India, Tibet, etc.) are descended from the Semitic. Their future depends on political considerations.

In Eastern Asia there are the complicated Chinese and Japanese systems of writing, which are not alphabetic. There has been agitation from time to time to abandon these in favor of the Latin alphabet. The movement has been particularly strong in Japan and has been dis-

cussed at times in the Japanese parliament.
There are difficulties in using the Latin alphabet to write Japanese, but it is felt that these
may be overcome. Recently it has been re-
ported in the newspapers that a system of Ro-
manizing Chinese writing has been perfected in
Leningrad and that it has aroused the interest
of the Chinese.

In the spread of the Latin alphabet two factors must be taken into account, national feeling and suitability. It is true that the Germans have maintained their Gothic form of the
Latin alphabet in preference to the humanistic
because of a feeling of nationalism, and that in
various countries there has been opposition to
the introduction of the Latin alphabet for the
same reason. But this feeling does not begin
to compare with that against the introduction
of some other language in place of the traditional language of the country. It is true also
that there has at times been dissatisfaction with
the Latin alphabet on account of various weaknesses, but again this dissatisfaction has not
been nearly as great as that with various existing languages as means of communication.
Thus it happens that fewer attempts have been
made to evolve new alphabets than to invent

new languages for international use. The chief arguments for artificial languages are greater simplicity and avoidance of national prejudices. It would be difficult to evolve a much simpler alphabet than the one we use, and the nationalistic opposition to the Roman alphabet is not strong enough to make the invention of a new alphabet desirable. We no longer think of our alphabet as the special property of any particular nation. As a matter of fact we may well say that in the matter of writing we have succeeded in making the Roman method universal, much as some persons advocate the use of the Latin language as a universal or international method of expression.

There are of course weaknesses in the alphabet, some of which are inherent in the alphabetical method of reproducing ideas. Phonetic alphabets have been devised as an improvement on the Roman alphabet in order to express accurately all the sounds of various languages, but these are scarcely practicable for general use. We apparently never will come to a system of writing which indicates pronunciation as accurately as a phonographic reproduction. This is not to say, however, that it might not be desirable to make improvements in our

[165]

alphabet from time to time, notably by the addition of a few characters.

The alphabet has always been in a stage of growth and it is to be hoped that it will continue to develop. At the present time it is highly desirable that it make progress along the line of legibility. The invention of printing, important as it was, has had the unfortunate effect of retarding the evolution of the alphabet, just as it has prevented, in English at least, spelling from keeping pace with pronunciation.

XIV. THE NAMES OF
THE LETTERS

TO THE Semites the names of the letters had a certain mnemonic value because they were words that meant something. To the Greeks, who took them over bodily, they had no meaning and were therefore cumbersome. Their only function was to show by their initial letters what sounds they represented. Meaningless names as different in length and sound as delta, mu, sigma, etc., were just as hard for the Greeks to memorize as for us.

The Etruscans seem not to have taken over this system of names when they adopted the Greek alphabet. It is not certain, however, whether they invented the new system which they handed down to the Romans and hence to us, or whether it is to be credited to the Greeks from whom they obtained the alphabet. In any case the new method is only a development of methods adopted by the Greeks. The system used for naming the five vowels was but an extension of that used by the Greeks in naming three of them (*e, o, u*), the last of which was a purely Greek name. The method of naming the mutes was that which the Greeks used in naming their new consonants (phi, chi, xi), in imitation of *p* ($\pi\epsilon\hat{\iota}$). Incidentally, we should say and write *xe, pe, phe, che, pse.* The forms *xi, pi,* etc., are due to the iotacism of modern Greek, which we long ago gave up in the pronunciation of ancient Greek, except, curiously, in the names of these letters.

The new system, as we know it in its earliest Roman form, is as follows:

(1) The names of the vowels consist merely of the vowel sounds: *a, e, i, o, u.*

(2) The liquids and nasals (*l, m, n, r*) and also *f, s,* and *x* are named in the same way as the vowels, by their own sounds.

(3) The other consonants, with the exception of *h, k, q,* consist of their own sounds followed by *e: be, ce,* etc.

According to some it was probably in the fourth century A.D. that the names of the letters in the second group acquired an *e* preceding their own sounds, but there is good reason for attributing this innovation to Varro. The letter names in their final Latin form were:

[168]

a, be, ce, de, e, ef, ge, ha, i, ka, el, em, en, o, pe, qu (pronounced *koo*), *er, es, te, u, ix, y* (French *u*), *zeta.*

The name *ha* (instead of *he*) has not been satisfactorily explained; possibly the influence of *ka* is responsible. The explanation of the names *ka* and *qu* has been given in Chapter IV: these letters were used only before *a* and *u* respectively. The name *ix* seems to have been *ex* at one time, but changed to *ix* under the influence of Greek *xi*. The Latin letter was not named *xe* or *xi*, probably because the Romans had difficulty (as we do) in pronouncing an *x* at the beginning of a word.

This system, which is a great improvement over the classical Greek method, was bequeathed by the Romans to the modern languages along with their alphabet. These names, in fact, have penetrated even to places which the Roman alphabet has failed to reach; Russians, for example, have in recent years adopted them for their letters, though the letters themselves are based directly on the Greek alphabet.

In English, we have kept most of the Latin names, changing only the pronunciation of them as we have changed the sounds of the letters

[169]

involved. It will be of interest to note the differences that have developed. The name *aitch* for *h* is derived from French *ache,* which, with Italian *acca* and other Romance forms, is thought to be derived from a Vulgar Latin (*h*)*ah* or (*h*)*ach*. The Germanic languages preserve the Latin name *ha*.

The name *ja*, like the letter, is new, made up apparently on the analogy of its neighbor *ka* in the seventeenth century. The name *ar* is due to the influence of *r*, which tends to make the preceding vowel less close, as in the British pronunciation of *Derby* as *Darby, clerk* as *clark* (cf. the family names *Darby, Clark*). The name *ve* is new, like the letter itself, made up on the analogy of the others in the seventeenth century. The name *double-u* indicates its origin: a double *u*, or rather *v*, going back to the time (seventh century) when these two letters were not differentiated. The name *wi* goes back to the Middle Ages and is said to be a combination of the two sounds (*u* and *i*) between which *y* (pronounced like French *u,* German *ü*) lay. The name *ze* is new, based on *be,* etc. In England it is still called *zed,* coming from zeta through the French. The old name *izzard* (cf. " from a to izzard ") is from

French *et zède* — from the custom of putting in an " and " before the last letter in reciting the alphabet.

It will not be without interest to mention a few of the peculiarities of the other modern languages. Spanish *jota* for *j* is derived from the Greek *iota;* cf. English *jot.* Italian *i lungo* for this letter describes the shape and perpetuates the name (*i longa*) used by the Romans for an *i* longer than usual to indicate quantitative length. German *jod* was taken from Hebrew *yod* in the sixteenth century, when *j* was first differentiated from *i.* In Italian, in which *k* is used only in foreign words, the Greek name *cappa* is used for that letter. German *fau* (*vau*) for *v* harks back to the original Semitic name of *f* or digamma and dates from the sixteenth century. German *ypsilon* and Italian *ipsilon* are modern adoptions of the Greek name for *y.* French *y grec* and Spanish *y griega* go back to a late Latin *y graeca;* the distinguishing adjective *graeca* was added when *y* lost its Greek sound and became identical with *i.* French *zède,* Italian *zeta,* German *zet* preserve the name *zeta.*

When we recapitulate the names chronologically we get a curious mixture: the name of *p* is

[171]

Semitic; the names of the Greek letters xi, phi, chi, psi are Greek, based on that of '*p;* the name of *e* was worn down by the Greeks from the Semitic *he,* and on this analogy *o* and *u* were named by the Greeks; named by a similar analogy, *a* and *i* are Etruscan, or possibly dialect Greek; *be, ce, de, ka, qu, te* are dialect Greek or Etruscan; *ha* is Etruscan or Roman; *ef, el, em, en, er, es* date from the end of the Roman Republic; *ex* may date from the same time, *ix* is later Roman; the original form of *zed* and the similar German and Romance names came into Latin from Greek at the end of the Republic; *aitch* and the Romance names for *h* go back to Vulgar Latin; the French and Spanish names of *y* are late Latin; *double-u* is Anglo-Saxon; *wi* is mediaeval; the various names of *j* and *v* belong to the sixteenth century; of these the German *jod* and *vau* were taken from the ancient Semitic. Thus the circle is complete: from Semitic back to Semitic in the course of perhaps thirty-five centuries!

The word " alphabet " preserves the Greek names of the first two letters, alpha, beta. The Romans thought that the word *elementa,* which they applied to the letters, was derived from *l, m, n.* While this popular etymology is now discredited, it is not without interest. In late antiquity we find the name *abecedarius,* based on the Latin names of the first four letters. In modern times we have come to use the familiar " a b c 's " and the more learned " abecedarium " or " abecedary."

XV. ABBREVIATIONS AND LIGATURES

THE NEED to save time and space leads not merely to changes in the forms of letters but to other important results. One is the production of abbreviations. Another is the development of ligatures, the tying together of letters in monogram forms which sometimes become abbreviations. Since the monumental work of Traube on the *Nomina Sacra* the importance of the study of abbreviations for the light they shed on the history of writing has been increasingly appreciated. They are as characteristic a feature of certain styles of script as the letter forms themselves.

Just as to-day we avoid abbreviations in formal writing and printing, just so they were avoided in the formal writing of antiquity and in most periods since. But they were necessary at times even in the most formal books and inscriptions, as at the end of a line when a word had to be completed. In informal writing their use varied according to circumstances. Naturally the secretary to whom letters were dictated or who took down the words of a speaker in the court or the senate developed them in the highest degree. Of the various systems of stenography in antiquity the best known was that devised by Tiro, the secretary of Cicero, and called *notae Tironianae,* Tironian notes.

The abbreviations used by the Romans may be grouped roughly into three classes: suspensions, contractions, and arbitrary signs. These classes continued to be used, with modifications, throughout the Middle Ages and have left interesting heritages in modern writing.

The most widely used form of abbreviation in the surviving documents of ancient Greece and Rome is suspension. By this we mean the use of the first letter or letters of the word. Such abbreviations, known in Latin as *litterae singulares* when a single letter was used, occur in thousands of examples in inscriptions, as may be seen from the indexes of the volumes of the *Corpus Inscriptionum Latinarum* or such handbooks as that by Egbert. Examples are B.M. for *bene merenti,* D.M. for *dis manibus,* H.M.H.N.S. for *hoc monumentum heredem non sequetur,* D.D.D. for *dono dedit dedicavit,* COS. for *cosul (consul),* AVG. for *Augustus.*

Of these D.D.D. is still used in the dedication of books. Other examples are the Roman *prae-nomina:* A., *Aulus;* L., *Lucius;* S. or Sex., *Sextus.* In some cases old forms of letters are used: ΛΛ for *Manius.* The use of C. for *Gaius* goes back to the time when C served for both *c* and *g* sounds. Possibly Ɔ for *centurio* or *cen-turia* originated in the time when writing was from right to left; more probably it was intro-duced at a later time but was suggested by the older form of writing.

Examples of suspension in English are of course very common. In Latin words and phrases used to-day we find such forms as e.g., *exempli gratia;* i.e., *id est;* sc., *scilicet;* etc., *et cetera;* ib. or ibid., *ibidem;* op. cit., *opere citato;* q.v., *quod vide;* s.v., *sub voce;* ad fin., *ad finem;* et al., *et alibi* or *et alii;* sup., *supra;* A.D., *anno Domini;* A.M., *ante meridiem;* Cu, *cuprum.* The period is normally used with both ancient and modern suspensions.

When the whole of the first syllable was em-ployed in suspension, it was not uncommon to include the first letter of the second syllable, as is true of some of the examples given above. Perhaps this led to the principle called syllabic suspension, by which the first letter of several

[176]

or all syllables is given. This became common in late antiquity and the Middle Ages. We have inherited this method of abbreviation in cf. for *confer;* lb. for *libra;* Sn for *stannum;* Ag for *argentum;* Pb for *plumbum,* etc.

When a single letter suspension was used, the plural was sometimes indicated by doubling: D., *dominus;* DD., *domini.* Occasionally the exact number was indicated by the number of letters and in that case doubling represented the dual: DD., *domini* (*duo*); DDD., *domini* (*tres*), DDDD., *domini* (*quattuor*). When more than one letter was used in suspension, the last was doubled to indicate the plural: COSS., *co*(*n*)*sules;* AVGG., *Augusti.* We still follow this practice in a number of abbreviations — English as well as Latin: LL.D., *Legum Doctor;* pp., pages (or Latin *paginae*); ff., following; sqq., *sequentes;* MSS., manuscripts; MM, *Messieurs.*

By contraction we mean the use of final letter, or letters, in addition to initial letter, or letters. The French abbreviation *Cie.* for *Compagnie* is a contraction, whereas the English *Co.* for *Company* is a suspension. The mediaeval abbreviation tm̄ sometimes stands for *tamen* and is then a syllabic suspension; but it also may mean *tantum*, and is thus a contraction. We may compare the suspension Penn. for Pennsylvania with the contraction Pa.; Penna. is a combination of the two. The system of contraction was an absolute necessity for the rapid writing of Greek and Latin, with their numerous inflectional endings. There are examples, though they are not numerous, in Greek inscriptions and papyri, and in Latin inscriptions. The Tironian notes show traces of them, and we may be sure on purely logical grounds that stenographic systems must have made large use of them. They did not, however, come into formal writing for some time. They may be thought of as purely cursive and informal, like the cursive letter forms, though even in cursive documents that have survived we do not find them frequently. There must be significance in the fact that the superscript *a*, used in the ancient *notae iuris* and in mediaeval contractions, is cursive in form.

The use of contractions was given an impetus from an unexpected quarter. In the Greek manuscripts of the Bible it became customary to write the name and titles of the Deity in a form imitative of the Hebrew method. The latter involved three points: the omission of vowels, which were never written in ancient Hebrew, the use of gold letters or other devices to make the name of the Deity stand out, just as we use a capital letter, and the use of a concealed form of the name of the Deity, known as the tetragram. At first the tetragram was preserved in Greek manuscripts; later the corresponding Greek word was used: $\overline{\Theta C}$ for θεός. Next came $\overline{KC}$ for κύριος, when it meant "Lord," but always written out in the sense of "lord." The line above was a differentiating mark. Soon there were added $\overline{IC}$ for 'Ιησοῦς and $\overline{XC}$ for Χριστός. Coming to be regarded as abbreviations, these last two signs were changed by conflation with the abbreviations by suspension of these words, i.e. $\overline{IC}$ was combined with IH to form $\overline{IHC}$, and $\overline{XC}$ with XP to form $\overline{XPC}$. Then $\overline{\Pi NA}$ was introduced for πνεῦμα in the sense of "holy spirit." By the fourth century four of these had been taken over into the Latin translations of the Bible: $\overline{\Theta C}$ became $\overline{DS}$ (deus) and $\overline{\Pi NA}$ became $\overline{SPS}$ (spiritus). $\overline{IHC}$ was taken over bodily with the mere change of the Greek C to S: $\overline{IHS}$. This eventually led to the spellings Ihesus and Hiesus when it was forgotten that H was the Greek eta (e) and not the Latin h. Fanciful

interpretations were later given to these letters: *in hoc signo* (*vinces*), which was Con-
stantine's motto, and *Iesus hominum salvator*.
$\overline{\text{XPC}}$ became $\overline{\text{XPS}}$. The suspended Greek
form XP was often used as a monogram, ✶,
and this too came over into Latin. The form
$\overline{\text{KC}}$ could not be represented by an identical
contraction of *dominus,* for that would be the
same as the one for *deus.* Eventually a combination of suspension and contraction led to
the forms $\overline{\text{DMS}}$ and $\overline{\text{DNS}}$. Later other ecclesiastical terms were treated in the same way
in both Greek and Latin, and finally the system
was extended to other words. At first dī̄s could
be used only of " God," while *deus* was " god."
In the end, dī̄s came to be used in both senses.

With the metamorphosis of the *nomina sacra*
into abbreviations there arose the custom, encouraged no doubt by the older use of contraction in stenographic and other rapid writing,
of changing the ending to show the case:
dī̄s, dī̄, dō̄, dm̄, etc.

Among the contractions of Latin words
used in English there are *ca.* for *circa;* No. for
numero; 4to for quarto, etc. The system is also
used in the half-Latin, half-English abbrevia-

tions, dwt. for *denarius* weight (*i.e.* penny-weight) and cwt. for *centum* weight (*i.e.* hundredweight). We likewise use contraction in purely English words, as in Wm. for William; bk. for book; hdkf. for handkerchief; Jr. for Junior; Mr. for Mister; Mme. for Madame; ft. for foot; acct. for account; atty. for attorney; Vt. for Vermont; Me. for Maine; Ga. and Va. for Georgia and Virginia. The contractions Ia. and Fla. have ousted the suspensions Io. and Flo.

The use of the line above the abbreviation originated in the desire to distinguish special characters and words from others. In both Greek and Latin it was written over the letters of the alphabet when used as numerals. It is found even with abbreviations by suspension in Latin as early as the second century, though we think of the dot as the typical sign for suspensions and the line for contractions. The latter remained as a typical abbreviation sign throughout the Middle Ages. Sometimes it was drawn through instead of above the letter, even in ancient inscriptions, as in the sign for *denarius* (✱), which is the numeral X with a line drawn through it. A relic of this sign is found in the abbreviation for pound sterling (£), which is an old-fashioned L with a line through it. This form came into existence at the end of the sixteenth century; before that the stroke was written to the right of the *l*. In most words the line (or "tittle" as it is called — from Latin *titulus*) has now been supplanted by the period, just as lb. is now much. more common than ℔ and ct. than ¢. The Spanish tilde (akin to "tittle") over an *n* gives that letter the sound of *ni* or *ny*, but the combination actually stands for *nn*, as in *año* from Latin *annus*. We have inherited it in "cañon," also spelled "·canyon." ℞ stands for *Recipe*, "Take," at the top of a prescription, and shows the abbreviation stroke. The common mediaeval abbreviation of *per* was p. ·This is preserved in our ℔, still to be found in the market reports of some of our newspapers. Our sign for "Number" (#) seems to be an *n* with a stroke through it. Since the sixteenth century we have also had the apostrophe, as in *o'er* for *over*, *isn't* for *is not*, *o'clock* for *of clock*, *let's* for *let us*.

What seem to be arbitrary signs are often conventionalized forms of letters, like some of the signs just mentioned. The Romans used Ɔ, a reversed C, as a symbol for various words, e.g. *centuria*. It also represented the syllable *con*, and this usage persisted throughout the Middle Ages. The Tironian notes in particular employed this and other symbols. Another that survived antiquity was 7, for *et*.

We have discussed ancient abbreviations from the standpoint of form. It is now necessary to say a word as regards usage. Ancient inscriptions and coins employ suspension for the most part, with the addition of a few symbols. Our earliest classical manuscripts have few abbreviations, and these are chiefly suspensions. Mention may be made here of the most common. The enclitic *-que* and the ending *-bus* are abbreviated Q· and B·; afterwards a colon or semicolon took the place of the dot. In later minuscule script the semicolon was written in one stroke and took on a form similar to our figure 3. This persisted even to the time of our first printed books. As it was similar to the modern cursive form of z, this letter was used for it. Hence our viz. for *vi(delicet)* and oz. for o(unce).

One other old abbreviation was the sign for M or N, at first confined to the end of a line when space ran out. This was a horizontal line above and after the last letter; later it was placed above the last letter. In form it was identical with the general sign of abbreviation.

In early theological manuscripts the *nomina sacra* were written in a special fashion that developed into a system of abbreviation. The Tironian notes consisted of all types of abbreviation, but we have no examples from ancient times. It is clear that technical treatises, especially in the law, made use of many abbreviations of all sorts, but not much of this material has come down to us, and we are forced to infer the extent of the use of such abbreviations from a study of later copies. It is probable that they were widely used. There is difference of opinion whether they originated in the law (the term *notae iuris* occurs) and spread to other fields, or whether they had a more general origin and received particular development in the important field of the law.

Out of the various systems described there arose the mediaeval system of abbreviations, with variations in the several countries. Their further history belongs to that of the national hands and their successors. We may summarize here as follows. In the earlier period abbreviations were used to the greatest extent in the Insular script. Later on many of these passed into the Continental scripts. That of Spain developed a system of its own in which the vowels were omitted. The Carolingian hand at the outset used abbreviations sparingly. With the coming of Gothic in the twelfth and thirteenth centuries the use of abbreviations reached a climax. The old abbreviations of whatever origin were freely used, and new ones were invented. One reason for this growth was the activity in the study of medicine, law, and philosophy in the universities. To this period we owe the use of superscript letters in abbreviations. It was not a new invention but an extension of earlier practice that, like most other things, had its origin in ancient times. Such types as 4th, M^r, D^o (for *ditto*), N^o (for *numero*), Rec^d, still common a generation ago, have all but disappeared with the advent of the typewriter. But we still use 8° (for octavo) and similar forms, in which the small letter is of course an *o*, the ending of the Latin ablative.

Humanistic writing was a return to Carolingian practice, not only in letter shapes but also in the relatively more sparing use of abbreviations, though they were by no means given up. Early printed books continued the use of the common abbreviations, such as the line for *m,* ꝗ for *-que,* etc. Gradually these were dispensed with, partly to improve the appearance of the page and partly to reduce the number of separate characters and thus to simplify composition. More recently editor and printer have for various reasons waged a relentless war upon all abbreviations. Ostensibly carried on in the interest of clearness this war has at times been carried to such absurd lengths as to lead to obscurity, *e.g.* when large numerals are spelled out instead of being indicated by the arabic symbols.

When two letters are written with a stroke or more in common, resembling Siamese twins, as it were, we call the combination a ligature. A complex or extended ligature of more than two letters is a monogram. Ligatures were frequently used to save time and space in ancient cursive writing, and some found their way even into formal capitals at the end of a line when space had to be conserved. The one most frequently used was NT in the form N̄.

But cursive influence did not make itself felt to any extent on the book hand in the matter of ligatures until the half-uncial came into use. The national hands which grew out of cursive preserved a still greater number of ligatures. The Carolingian script suppressed most of them; at Tours indeed the scribes eliminated all of them for a time. But some of them were too well established and therefore have persisted to this day. The most important of all was that of *et*, introduced into formal writing by half-uncial. We use it in English for " and," the equivalent of Latin *et*, and call it " ampersand " ("and per se and "), a name that arose when this character was placed at the end of the alphabet and was recited with the other letters: "x, y, z, and, per se [by itself] (the character standing for) and." This has taken on many different forms in different styles of writing and printing, but nearly all are based on the old & and the italic *&*.

Other ligatures still in use are *ae* (æ), *oe* (œ), *ct* (with a connecting stroke either round at the top or more or less straight: ᴄᴛ, *ct*), *ff*, *fi*, *ffi* (without a dot; these ligatures are obligatory in modern fonts), *fl* (*fl*), *ffl* (*ffl*), *ss* (ß), *st* (with round or long *s:* ſt, ſt, ſt). There is also the sign @, which is really for *ad*, with an exaggerated uncial *d*.

[187]

In ancient times monograms were used especially on coins, where space was greatly restricted. In the modern world we find them on the titlepages of books as publishers' devices, on stationery, jewelry, purses, handkerchiefs.

XVI. NUMERALS

THE TERM "Roman" numerals be-
trays their origin. They are themselves of two different types. The
numerals I, V, X are older than the alphabet
in Italy and are distinct from it. They belong
to the realm of finger counting, which throughout Roman history, clear up to the days of the
Venerable Bede, remained an important method
of calculation, made necessary by the much
more difficult character of Roman counting
caused by the lack of a zero. I simply represents a single finger or digit (*digitus,* "finger"). II, III, IIII (which was the earlier
way of indicating four) represent the number
of fingers. V is the open palm — one side rep-
resenting the thumb, the other the four fingers.
VI, etc., are natural combinations by addition.
X represents two hands. The analogy of II,
etc., led to the use of XX, etc. These three
symbols really belong to the primitive type of
pictographic writing. The addition method of

obtaining such forms as IIII, VIIII, etc., is older than the subtraction method which is now general in IV, IX, etc. An instance of the older method may still be seen on clock and watch dials in the use of IIII instead of IV. Both methods were used by the Romans, who went even farther than we do in the application of the subtraction method, by occasional use of such forms as IIX for 8. The suggestion of the subtraction method no doubt came from such usages as *duodcviginti*, " two from twenty," as the designation for eighteen. It gained favor because it saved space. It will be noted that in the course of time I, V, X became identical in form with three letters of the alphabet. They bear, however, no relation whatever to these letters. The numeral V, for example, is not, strictly speaking, the letter V.

The higher numerals came in with the alphabet, as we have seen. The letters for which the Romans had no use were adapted to this purpose. The Western Greek Ѱ (chi) was used for 50. This form and variations of it, such as ⊥, were used until the second century A.D. As the form ⊥ sometimes was used for the letter L, numeral and letter gradually were confused and became identical in form. The process was no doubt aided by the fact that the numerals I, V, and X had become identical in shape with letters of the alphabet. It is a curious fact that V̇, like V, was derived from a picture of the open hand. It is still more curious that they are so closely related in numerical value (5, 50) as well as in origin.

Greek Θ was used for 100. At an early date its form had been modified to the point that it was subject to the influence of the initial letter of *centum* and was thereafter written C, the only form that we actually find in Roman times. Φ became 1000. Its shape changed to ⊕ and later to ∞ or CⅠↃ. The last form is sometimes found in books printed a few centuries ago. At the same time *mille* was sometimes abbreviated M when it stood for *mille passus*. Only after Roman times did M supplant ∞. The process was helped by the uncial form of M: ⓜ.

To obtain 500, the Romans took half of the 1000 symbol: D, ⅠↃ. Once again the numeral coincided with a letter of the alphabet. Thus all seven of the Roman numerals now have the shapes of letters, but only two of them, C and M, bear any sort of relation to the letters with which they are expressed.

[191]

It will be noted that the Greek method of using the letters of the alphabet as numerals [33] (as we sometimes use A, B, C for 1, 2, 3) was not used by the Romans. Probably this was due to the fact that they (or rather the Etruscans from whom they received both numerals and alphabet) already possessed I, V, and X. They did, however, accept the Greek principle in a way, by using the idle Greek letters for the higher numbers.

The assimilation of form of the numerals to certain of the letters was a disadvantage in that it sometimes led to ambiguity. Hence it became customary to write a horizontal line through or above the numerals. Thus the *sesterius,* consisting of $2\frac{1}{2}$ *asses,* was first written as IIS (i.e. *duo* and *semis*), later as HS, and this remained the fixed form. In general, however, the practice of writing the distinguishing line above, rather than through, the numeral became more common. In writing we use a similar method of distinguishing numerals from letters, by lines at the upper and lower end (*e.g.* XIII, not XIII). Perhaps this practice is an inheritance of the Roman custom.

The question of the so-called Arabic numerals is not a simple one. According to the most generally accepted view they originated in India. The beginning of the system may be seen there on inscriptions of the third century B.C. But the early examples have no zero, and without the zero the Hindu-Arabic system is no better than the Roman or any other. The zero does not make its appearance until the ninth century A.D., though it probably existed earlier, but even before that the people of India had made an important step in giving "place values" to the numerals. The place value makes it possible for a given numeral to represent not only itself, but in combination with other numerals, ten times itself, a hundred times itself, etc.; so in 6876 the last 6 represents itself, the first one 6000.

The Arabs took over the Indian system in the eighth century and passed it on to Europe through Spain. But for many centuries it made little headway in Europe. Gerbert, who became Pope Sylvester II in 999, knew the numerals from 1–9 but not the zero, which began to be used in the eleventh or twelfth century. Leonardo Fibonacci of Pisa, writing at the beginning of the thirteenth century, was the first to set forth the advantages of the new system.

But there is another theory of the origin of the numerals. They are mentioned in a work on geometry attributed to Boethius, who lived in the fifth and sixth centuries. Those who consider this work genuine say that the signs were invented by the Neo-Pythagoreans and passed from Greece to Persia and from Persia to India and the Arabs. But many doubt the genuineness of the Boethian geometry and attribute it to the eleventh century. A compromise theory is that Boethius and the Neo-Pythagoreans got the numerals from India. In any case, the really important element, the zero, seems to have been an Indian invention.

The forms of the Arabic numerals have been variously explained, but no complete explanation has found general acceptance. The first three developed from horizontal lines indicating the number involved: $-$ $=$ $\equiv$. The figures 2 and 3 were formed by writing the strokes without lifting the pen, just as Roman II and III were often written u or ɯ in the Middle Ages.

A word may be added in regard to the various mathematical signs. According to some, the plus sign ($+$) is derived from the ligature & for *et*, but this is uncertain. It and the minus

(−) sign first appear in the fifteenth century. The square root sign (√) is nothing but the letter *r*, standing for *radix*, " root." Similarly the integral (∫) is only the old long *s*, the initial of *summa*, " sum " of the differentials.

XVII. WRITING MATERIALS
AND PRACTICES

FROM early times stone and metals have
been important mediums for monumental
writing. But for other kinds of writing
a more convenient and less cumbersome medium
was necessary. At an early period two main
varieties became the most common. The Baby-
lonians scratched their ideas on clay tablets
which were then baked. Such tablets were occasionally used by the Greeks and Romans. We
recall also the use of potsherds, *ostraca,* from
which is derived the word "ostracism" because with them the Greeks voted on banish-
ment. The Egyptians very early discovered a
much better plan, that of cutting the stalks of
the papyrus plant lengthwise into thin strips
which were then formed into sheets by placing
a number of strips side by side and another
layer crosswise. Pressing and beating of the
strips while moist made the strips adhere to one
another because of the sticky nature of the
pith, though some maintain that a paste was

used.³⁴ The sheets were then pasted end to end in rolls. As Egypt was almost the only place where the papyrus plant grew, this country remained the center of the papyrus trade throughout antiquity. The word papyrus is probably Egyptian. Another name used by the Greeks was βύβλος, derived from the Syrian city Byblus, a center of the papyrus trade. From this came the word βιβλίον, " book," whence the English " Bible." To-day an inferior variety of papyrus grows near Syracuse, in Sicily, and papyrus sheets are being manufactured there as a curiosity. The plant has disappeared from Egypt.

Papyrus was the chief writing material of Greece and Rome. Writing was done with a reed pen (*calamus*) and ink made of the liquid of the cuttlefish or of soot or other ingredients. The Egyptians used reeds with frayed edges resembling brushes. This may have been the early Greek and Roman method, but the reed of the classical period was split like our pen.

Next in importance to papyrus in Greece and Rome was the wax tablet. This was made of wood covered with a thin coating of wax in which letters were scratched with a pointed stylus of some hard substance, usually bone or bronze. The other end was blunt and was used to smooth the wax surface, *i.e.* to erase the writing. The wax tablet resembled a modern school slate. Sometimes two (or more) were fastened together, like double slates. Wax tablets were used chiefly for temporary writing, such as letters, accounts, etc. Such tablets continued to be used to some extent throughout the Middle Ages and even into the nineteenth century.

But other materials served for writing surfaces besides papyrus and tablets of wax. The story of the Sibyl points to the utilization of leaves, as in other parts of the world, *e.g.* India. The etymology of the Latin word *liber* shows that bark was employed in early times. In fact it continued in use well into the historical period. Every schoolboy is familiar with the use of birch bark; in Rome the inner bark of the linden tree was the favorite.

Another material employed from an early period was the skin of animals. While its use was widespread, its real popularity began in Asia Minor, where improved methods of preparation were developed. The word " parchment " is derived from the Latin *pergamena*, itself a derivative of Pergamum, the center of the parchment trade, just as the Greeks got their name for papyrus (βύβλος) from Byblus. The rivalry of papyrus and parchment is well illustrated by the story that in the second century B.C. Ptolemy, king of Egypt, put an embargo on the shipment of papyrus to Pergamum because he did not want Eumenes II, king of that city, to build a library which would rival the famous one at Alexandria, and that for this reason Eumenes was forced to use parchment. Whatever truth there may be in the story, it indicates that parchment began to be an important article at this period and that it grew in importance whenever the supply of papyrus was low. The earliest Greek parchment in existence dates from about 189 B.C., when, curiously enough, Eumenes II was king at Pergamum. It was found at Doura-Europos on the Euphrates in 1923.[35]

By the first century A.D. parchment was a common material in Rome, as we know from Martial. The Roman parchment book was not a roll, like that of papyrus but, based on the form of the wax tablet, it took on the shape that has persisted in our modern books. In fact parchment apparently first came into general use in Rome as a substitute for wax in small tablets.

[199]

The name codex, given to a book not in roll
form, was originally applied to two or more
tablets, fastened together. To Rome, then,
we owe the form of the modern book. The importance of this invention can hardly be over-
estimated; the enormous development of modern bookmaking would have been impossible
without it, and printing would have remained a
relatively unimportant art. The codex had the
advantage of compactness and was preferred
for traveling copies. Parchment was used on
both sides, while in the case of papyrus the
writing generally covered one side only. Parchment was favored because it was more durable;
it also was easier to write on, and the writing
was easier to read. The codex was much more
convenient. It could be referred to more easily — an important consideration when the literature had attained large proportions. Technical works in particular, such as legal treatises,
had to be consulted, not read. It is significant that *the* book in the new form was the
codex, or code, of laws. Why then was not
papyrus used in this form? It was eventually
so used to some extent but apparently was not
considered strong enough since we find manuscripts made of papyrus in which there are oc-

casional parchment leaves to give strength. But the real point is that we have two sets of things contending for mastery: papyrus and parchment, roll and codex. As between the latter two there was no question as to the ultimate outcome: conservatism might prolong the use of the former, but the advantages of the latter clearly predicted its eventual triumph. But as between the two writing materials the outcome depended in part on economic factors: if the supply of papyrus had remained plentiful and its price much lower, the papyrus codex would have been the regular thing at least for ordinary books. As it is, parchment gradually became more and more common and by the fourth century it was dominant. Christianity did much to spread its use, for the Bible, *i.e.* the Book, was the core of the new religion and had to be durable. Parchment became the chief writing material of the Middle Ages. Papyrus however continued to be used sporadically even to the eleventh century. The use of the roll (of parchment or paper) never died out completely; certain kinds of records are still kept in this form in England. About the same time that parchment triumphed over papyrus, the pen (in its proper sense of quill, from *penna,*

" feather ") supplanted the reed, though the latter was occasionally used as late as the fifteenth century, as it still is in India and elsewhere. Bronze pens also were used by the Romans.

Parchment was made chiefly of the skins of sheep, goats, and calves. The skin of young animals gave a finer parchment which we call vellum. Even uterine vellum was used from the thirteenth century on.

The papyrus roll was then the chief material of Greece and republican Rome, while the parchment codex was that of the later Empire and the Middle Ages. Each had its influence on the development of writing and writing practices. Thus the roll with its standard lengths led to division of literary productions into books. The Alexandrian scholars arbitrarily divided the *Iliad* and the *Odyssey* into books. Virgil, on the other hand, used the book division to make artistic units of his *Aeneid*. The parchment book made possible the use of shading in writing, especially after the introduction of the quill pen. To parchment we owe the preservation of much ancient literature which would have been lost if copied only on the relatively short-lived papyrus.

Paper, made of rags, hemp, etc., was invented

by the Chinese in the second century. The Arabs adopted it in the eighth century and brought knowledge of it to Europe. The name paper shows that papyrus was still known when the new material was introduced. We have a Greek manuscript written on paper in the eighth or ninth century, but the use of this material did not become common in Greece until the thirteenth century. In Western Europe there are documents on paper dating from the early twelfth century. But the new material was not used in books to any extent until the fourteenth century and did not become a serious rival of parchment until the fifteenth.

The papyrus roll was covered with a gaily colored piece of parchment. This material is still used for binding, and the bright colors linger too. The codex was bound in wooden boards, for which the modern "boards" are a lighter and cheaper substitute. Even in late antiquity the binding of the codex was often very elaborate; cloth and leather, painting and precious stones helped to make it so. The rolls, called *volumina*, whence our "volumes," were placed in boxes, usually cylindrical, called *capsae* or *scrinia*. The grouping of the books of Livy in decades is due to the fact that ten books were kept in each *capsa*. Tags or tickets giving the name of author and title were tied to the end of the roll. These correspond to the labels on the backs of modern books.

For erasing, the sponge was applied to both papyrus and parchment. On the latter the knife was also used, especially for short corrections. Sometimes, on account of the expense or scarcity of writing material, whole manuscripts were erased and a new work was copied on them. Such palimpsests, as they are called, are especially common on parchment, on which erasing was easier. Almost always traces of the original writing remain to a greater or lesser extent. Thus valuable old manuscripts have been preserved to us, in some cases furnishing our only text for certain ancient works, as Cicero's *De re publica*, Fronto, and Gaius. There are even a few examples of "codices ter scripti," manuscripts used three times.

In papyrus manuscripts the horizontal grain of the writing material was generally a sufficient guide for the scribe in keeping the lines straight, but ruling with lead (not of course the graphite of "lead" pencils) was sometimes practised. Ruling was regularly done on parchment, and traces of it may be found in many manuscripts. It was customary also to rule vertically for the margins. To mark off the places where lines were to be drawn tiny holes were pricked. In early codices a hard point was used in ruling, and several leaves were ruled at a time. From the eleventh century ruling was again done with lead.

Several sheets of parchment were laid together and folded once to form the writing unit, or gathering. Usually four sheets, making eight folios, or leaves (sixteen pages), were put together to form a *quaternio,* whence our word "quire," now used for any combination of sheets folded together. The sheets were so laid that the flesh side of one sheet was opposite the flesh side of another. Our books are still made in quires, but the sheets of paper are larger and are folded more times, so that a single sheet makes as many as eight quires. The binding term "folio" goes back to the time when a sheet was folded only once.

The folding kept together the sheets of the quire before binding, but some device was necessary to insure that the quires be bound in the right order. From an early period the quires received signatures, as they are called, sometimes at the beginning, but usually at the bottom of the last page. These consisted of consecutive numbers or letters. After the eleventh century the first word or words of the next gathering were used as signatures. This custom was extended in the fifteenth century to every leaf or page and is found in many printed books down to the eighteenth century. The earlier signature by numbers or letters was never entirely given up and is still used in printed books, though the practice changed back to putting the indications on the first page of the quire. The additional numbering of leaves within the quire began in the fourteenth century and was continued in early printed books. Many books today have the second leaf of the quire numbered, *e.g.* C ii or E 2, or 6*. The consecutive numbering of leaves throughout is found from the thirteenth century on. The modern practice is to number the leaves or folios (not the pages) of manuscripts and to refer to the two sides as r(ecto) and v(erso). The numbering of pages instead of leaves began in the fifteenth century but was not firmly established until the sixteenth.

Large codices were usually written in two, sometimes three or even four columns. The Codex Sinaiticus of the Bible is in four columns, so that the open book, with its eight columns side by side, gives the impression of a roll, whence the custom of writing in columns obviously arose.

In early Greek manuscripts a horizontal line or other mark was made below the beginning of a line in which a paragraph ended. Then it became customary to make larger the first letter of the first complete line of the new paragraph and to let it project into the margin. The beginning of the practice may be seen in first-century papyri. In Latin manuscripts, even in early cursive documents, a new line was started for the new paragraph, and a larger, projecting letter was used. Examples from inscriptions go back to the first century B.C. Sometimes the paragraph mark was also used. It took the form Γ, from which our ¶ is derived.

From early times it was customary to begin a page or column in Latin codices with a larger letter, sometimes in color. Later this custom died out, but the initial letters of books and chapters were elaborately colored — illuminated, we say. Pictures and designs of various sorts were employed. Red, blue, and gold were the favorite colors. The old custom of illumination is still continued by us. *De luxe* editions have colored initials, other books have large initials at the beginning of chapters. It is no longer as common as it was a generation or two ago to use actual pictures or intricate designs for initial letters.

Sentences were early separated by a larger space than words, as is still done. As early as the sixth century we find larger letters used at the beginning of sentences. This is but an outgrowth of an old practice of beginning a new line with every sentence, as some writers to-day make every sentence a paragraph, and of using larger letters at those points. It was not long before these larger letters were capitals, not merely a larger size of the text script.

The use of letters of various sizes and styles for different lines is of ancient origin. Inscriptions show many interesting and complex examples of it, including the use of square and rustic capitals on the same stone. In the earliest Latin manuscripts written in capitals there are running heads in smaller capitals. In uncial manuscripts these heads are often written in smaller uncial but sometimes in square or rustic capitals. That marked the beginning of the custom of employing the older scripts for heading, titles, colophons, and first lines. In manuscripts written in Carolingian minuscules (especially at Tours) we find square and rustic capitals, uncials, and half-uncials for different sorts of headings, initials, and special material. In such practices we find the beginning of our employment of different fonts of type together.

The use of older scripts for titles, etc., and of larger letters for initials gave rise to our distinction between capital and small letters. We are apt to think of our present practice as definitive and clear-cut, which it is not at all. It is simply the present stage of a usage which has slowly evolved through many centuries and which is subject to constant change. An examination of other steps in the process will make this clear.

The employment of capital letters at the beginning of each line of poetry began as early as the eighth century. The purpose was to make clear that the content was in verse. Other assisting devices were to leave a letter space after the first letter and to draw a colored line (usually red) through the initial. The writing of verses on separate lines was an ancient practice in Greece and Rome.

In the discussion of abbreviations mention was made of the device of giving prominence to

the name of the Deity by a stroke written above.
In Latin manuscripts the same distinction was
sometimes given to Greek or other foreign
words. In Greek manuscripts of the tenth
century and later we find strokes over proper
names. In a sixth-century Latin manuscript
proper names are often indicated by dots after
them. By the eleventh century we find capitals
used for the initials of many important words.
An additional method of giving prominence was
to draw a red line through the initial, just as we
saw was done in the first letter of a line of poetry. The custom of capitalizing becomes more
common in the thirteenth century. The capi-
talization of names is sporadic thereafter and
does not become truly fixed until the sixteenth
century though some fourteenth-century manuscripts make a regular feature of it. For a long
time other important words besides names were
capitalized and still are to a certain extent
though the tendency is to reduce their number.
German is the most conservative of the modern
languages in this respect, as it is in the continued
use of the Gothic script, for it capitalizes all
nouns. English is alone in capitalizing proper
adjectives. A recent fad eliminates capitals
even in proper names and at the beginning of

sentences. This device, intended to catch the reader's eye, is an interesting reversion to the original use of a single style of letters.

The illumination of initials was not the only coloring done in manuscripts. The word *rubrica* (whence our "rubric"), derived from *ruber*, "red," indicates clearly enough that the Romans used red in titles. We find red titles in Greek and Latin manuscripts of all periods. The writing of titles and other red ink matter was usually done by a special rubricator. He was sometimes followed by an illuminator who did the elaborate miniatures. As a guide to the rubricator the scribe put catch-titles in small faint letters in the margin, and catch-letters for the initials. Sometimes these were erased, covered over, or trimmed off but in many manuscripts they are still visible.

In the earliest manuscripts the text is usually written continuously without separation of words. This practice has sometimes been misinterpreted by philologists as having something to do with word and sentence grouping. The reason for it apparently was the feeling that spaces at uneven intervals marred the beauty of the line. In some early manuscripts words are separated by dots as in inscriptions. It is significant that in the earliest cursive writing separation is much more frequent. In fact it was the cursive influence that eventually led to regular separation. It becomes somewhat pronounced in the national hands, but Carolingian script is the first to make it an established practice. The actual space left is sometimes slight; the significant point is that words are not joined by ligatures or otherwise. Naturally there was much variation: prefixes and prepositions tended to be treated alike, both detached or (and this was much more common) both attached. In Greek manuscripts separation first appears with some regularity in ninth-century minuscule, possibly through Carolingian influence.

In English we still are uncertain in our practice in regard to separation. We compromised by introducing the hyphen in some cases and thereby made matters worse, for we now have three ways of writing certain words, e.g. *inkpot, ink-pot, ink pot*. We also have such monstrosities (if the reader will permit a personal prejudice) as *nonco-operative*.

Punctuation was used from early times, though sparingly at first. We hear of a system worked out in the third century B.C. by Aristophanes of Byzantium, but there are traces of punctuation in still earlier Greek papyrus fragments. Such punctuation as there is in the papyri consists of a high point, at the top of the line of writing, for a full stop. This is found also in early codices, together with a middle point, which serves for lighter punctuation. Eventually the latter becomes a low point, like our period. The ninth century, so important for Greek writing, marks the introduction of comma and question mark.

Breathings and accents also go back to Aristophanes and other Alexandrian scholars but are rarely seen in the extant papyri. The rough and smooth breathings are the left and right halves respectively of H: ⊦ ⊣. The modern rounded forms that look like single quotation marks did not become established until the eleventh century though there are examples in ancient inscriptions. Accents are not frequent in papyri until the third century A.D. and in parchment codices not until the eighth or ninth.

Long and short marks, hyphens, and apostrophes also go back to Hellenistic times and are occasionally seen in papyri. Other signs to be noted in papyri are marks of diaeresis, in various forms (chiefly like the modern) and quota-

tion marks, especially in the form < or >, though
the apostrophe form of modern single quotation
marks is found early. Sometimes the quotation
marks are repeated before every line, as is still
done in some European countries, and as was
the practice in English books as late as the early
nineteenth century. The asterisk (*) and obe-
lisk (†) also were among the critical signs of the
Alexandrians but they are rare in manuscripts.

In early Latin manuscripts little punctuation is found, though we know that the Greek
system of points was familiar to the Romans.
Some of the early codices in capitals have punctuation but it was added later. In early uncial
manuscripts the point is used for a half stop,
and the colon or colon with dash for a full stop.
Later the comma, in the form of a slanting line,
was used like the point. The semicolon, in the
form of a dot and a slanting line, came in with
the sixth century; an inverted form did not become common until the eighth. The question
mark is first found in the same century. At
first it looks something like a prostrate S, then
it becomes semi-erect, and finally stands upright
— thus portraying the evolution of homo sa-
piens himself. Quotation marks at first were
like those in Greek (>), a form now used in

some European type fonts. Then they were rounded and resembled a slender S. With the clipping of one curve our modern form was achieved in the sixth century. Double quotation marks occur as early as the seventh century. In imitation of Greek practice *h* is sometimes indicated by the rough breathing in its original angular form from the ninth to the fifteenth century. The hyphen becomes frequent in the eleventh century; before that a dot was occasionally used.

Our punctuation is still in a state of flux but the system in vogue goes back in its essential form to sixteenth-century Italy: to a treatise written by Aldus Manutius, grandson of the famous early Venetian printer of the same name.

It should be remembered that the ancients made up for lack of punctuation by other devices. So the Romans used -*ne* instead of a question mark (cf. the inverted question mark at the beginning of a sentence in modern Spanish) and often used *at* for quotation marks in the sense " but you say."

At the beginning of a Latin manuscript it was customary to prefix to the title the word *incipit*, " there begins." At the end we again find the

[215]

title, with the word *explicit*, an abbreviated form of *explicitus*, "unrolled," derived from the papyrus roll, which was ended when unrolled. A variant for *explicit* is *finit*. Our *finis* is a more modern variant, probably not antedating the fifteenth century.

It was unfortunately not the regular practice to indicate date and place of writing, though there are many Greek and Latin manuscripts (especially the former) in which this is done. When given, the date is at the end, and the scribe sometimes adds his name and many interesting data, such as the completion of the task at night or on some holiday or other important occasion, or that he is not responsible for the mistakes, or that he wrote with his left hand, etc. Most frequent is an expression of thanks, often obviously from the heart, that the work was finished, such as *Deo gratias amen*. The frequent use of *feliciter* goes back to antiquity.

XVIII. OUR DEBT

WE HAVE seen that we owe the alphabet to the Semites, the vowels to the Greeks, and the letter forms as well as the transmission of the alphabet to the Romans. One glance at other modern forms of Semitic script such as Hebrew and Arabic, and even at Greek writing is sufficient to convince us of the surpassing importance of the Roman contribution.

Our use of capitals as distinguished from small letters started with the ancient practice of beginning a book, chapter, or page with a larger letter. Our use of different fonts of type for differentiation began with the running heads of ancient manuscripts and was carried further in Carolingian times, especially at Tours.

Thus the use of capitals by the side of small letters was a gradual evolution out of practices originating in antiquity. The shapes of our modern capitals are for the most part derived directly or indirectly from ancient inscriptions.

We constantly go back to them for inspiration, as did the scribes of ninth-century Tours. " The twenty or so forms, usually called ' square capitals ' have come down to us, as it were, from heaven, and we can meddle with them only at the peril of being both illegible and inartistic." [36] Numerous varieties, many ancient or mediaeval, may be seen. V is often used for U, as in antiquity. Sometimes certain letters, like T or I, are taller. The centered separation point of Latin inscriptions is also to be seen in modern inscriptions and display advertisements. The use of serifs in both capital and small letters is derived from the ancients.

Our small letters go back, as we have seen, to fifteenth-century revivals and modifications of ninth-century Carolingian letters, which in turn are based on ancient cursive and half-uncial. Especial attention may be called to certain points. The *a* of roman type goes back to uncial, due to its resurrection by Carolingian scribes; the italic *a* is that of cursive and half-uncial. The small *e* sometimes is double, like two *c*'s, one above the other, in mediaeval fashion. The letter *g* still shows its cursive origin in the useless tail at the upper right. This appendage was very helpful in the time when this

letter was attached thereby to a following letter. The dots of *i* and *j* are mediaeval. The
usual *s* is the round variety, but the long *s*,
similar to the *f*, is still seen occasionally in special types, used in display advertisements. It
was still used regularly in the first edition of the
Encyclopaedia Britannica (1768) except at the
end of a word. It is likewise common in current German fonts of roman type. The old
practice of using long and round *s* together at
the end of a word is preserved not only in the
roman type of Germany but occurs also (in a
ligatured form) in the letterhead of the Claren-
don Press of Oxford. Some people still use it
in the word " Miss " when addressing an enve-
lope. Sometimes *w* consists of two overlap-
ping, instead of contiguous, *v*'s, as in the olden
days.

Older styles of letters are not uncommon.
The Gothic, or Old English, is of course the
most frequently used. It is a favorite for the
names of newspapers, as 𝔗𝔥𝔢 𝔑𝔢𝔴 𝔜𝔬𝔯𝔨 𝔗𝔦𝔪𝔢𝔰,
𝔆𝔥𝔦𝔠𝔞𝔤𝔬 𝔇𝔞𝔦𝔩𝔶 𝔗𝔯𝔦𝔟𝔲𝔫𝔢, 𝔅𝔬𝔰𝔱𝔬𝔫 𝔈𝔳𝔢𝔫𝔦𝔫𝔤 𝔗𝔯𝔞𝔫-
𝔰𝔠𝔯𝔦𝔭𝔱. It is a natural type for the official name
of the University of Chicago, with its Gothic
architecture. It is also appropriate for articles
whose names include " Old English " or some-

thing similar. Otherwise it is used for purely ornamental purposes. Its association with Christmas may be partly due to the German origin of some of the characteristics of that holiday.

Not a few ligatures may be found in current printing. Our system of abbreviation is Roman and mediaeval and preserves many actual relics of earlier days. Punctuation began in antiquity. The names of our letters are for the most part ancient. Roman numerals live up to their name. To Rome we owe the present convenient form of our books.

How common old practices still are may be seen by a glance at the advertising pages of our magazines, with their wealth of type fonts. One number of *The National Geographic Magazine* revealed, among other things, various forms of the & ligature; centered dots, round and triangular, between words as in ancient inscriptions; heavily shaded letters; a Visigothic *g;* a *t* with the cross stroke looped to the left, in one case actually touching the line of writing as in various mediaeval scripts; capitals imitating the triangular cut letters of Roman inscriptions; a nearly uncial *d;* a large capital as an initial and smaller capitals for the rest of the first word of a paragraph; a very elaborate initial of late Gothic design.

The importance of writing and especially of the alphabet cannot be exaggerated. Art, culture, religion, politics, commerce, language, all are related and indebted to the alphabet. The progress of art and culture can be traced in the history of writing. Our civilization could hardly have advanced as far as it has, or in the same way, without the alphabet. Religious differences in Jugoslavia are marked by the use of two alphabets. The spirit of nationalism causes Germany to preserve its Gothic writing and Ireland its early script. How commerce has been facilitated by the alphabet can hardly be estimated; if commerce follows the flag, the alphabet precedes both. The elimination of three letters from the Bulgarian alphabet in 1922 led to the resignation of two ministers and wide dissatisfaction. The adoption of the Roman alphabet gave Turkey a definite trend toward Western civilization.

It is interesting to see how closely the development of the English language parallels that of the script in which it is written. The Saxons came into contact with the Latin language and Italian script when still in Germany. But the

Saxon language was influenced only slightly by this contact, and the writing borrowed from Italy was so completely naturalized that we think of the runes as a Germanic national alphabet. The coming of Augustine from Rome brought Christian words into the Saxon language and the Christian half-uncial for its writing. The language was appreciably influenced but not changed by this event; the writing was thoroughly assimilated and nationalized. The Norman Conquest profoundly altered the old Saxon language; the new Carolingian script which the Normans brought was used in writing the changing tongue. For several hundred years thereafter the English language and script were greatly affected by France. Thus the Saxon and the Norman French eventually merge into Chaucerian English, written in the French Gothic hand. Finally the language of England again underwent deep changes as a result of the Italian Renaissance, which brought with it the humanistic writing and printing of Italy. Thus pagan Italy, Christian Rome, Carolingian and Gothic France, and Renaissance Italy have left their impress on the writing as on the language of England.

The movement for an international language,

whether an existing one like Latin or an artificial one, has not met with much success. On the other hand, the Roman alphabet has become truly international. It is a splendid example for those interested in international cooperation to keep before their eyes. Though the sword of Rome has failed, its pen has triumphed.

INDEX OF PLATE DESCRIPTIONS

a

b

c

PLATE I

a

b

c

PLATE II

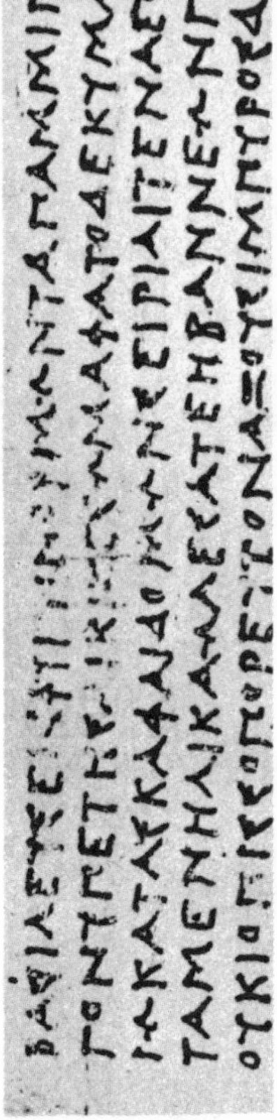

a

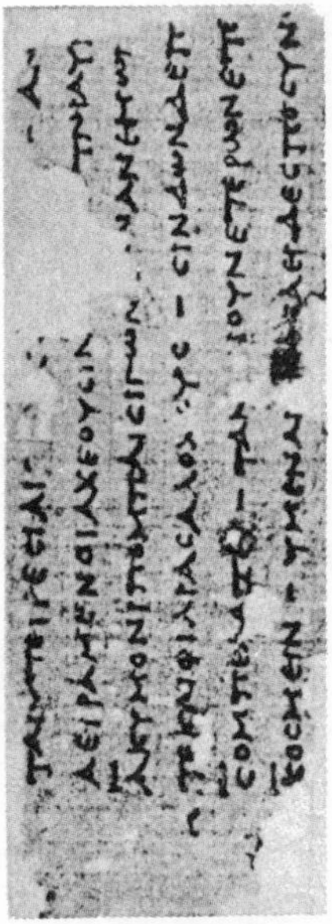

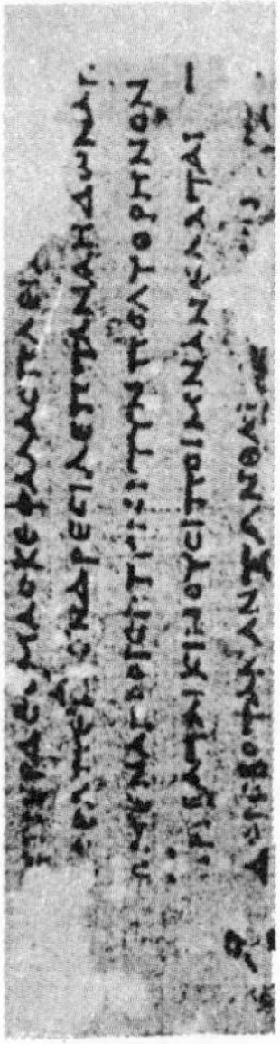

b

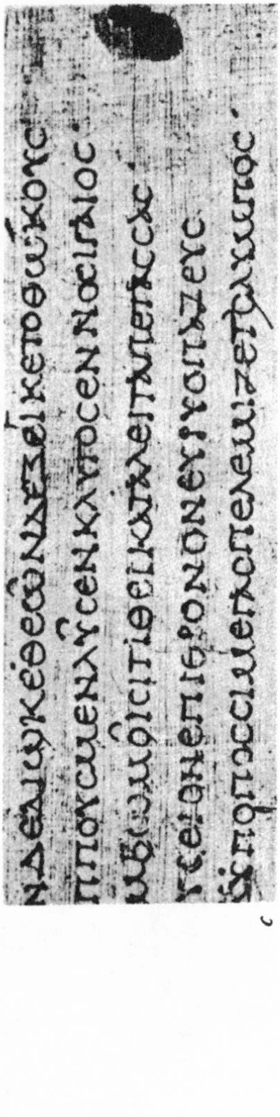

c

PLATE III

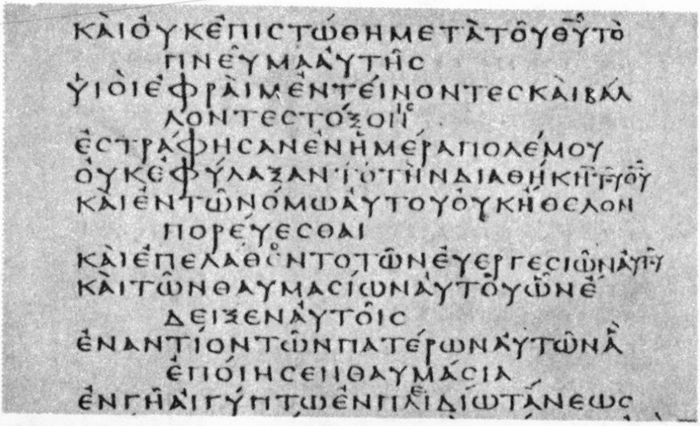

a

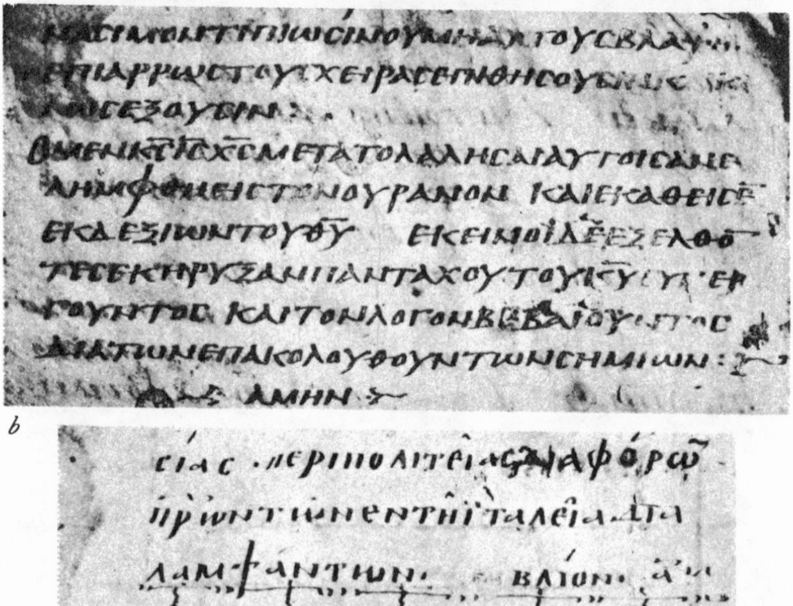

b

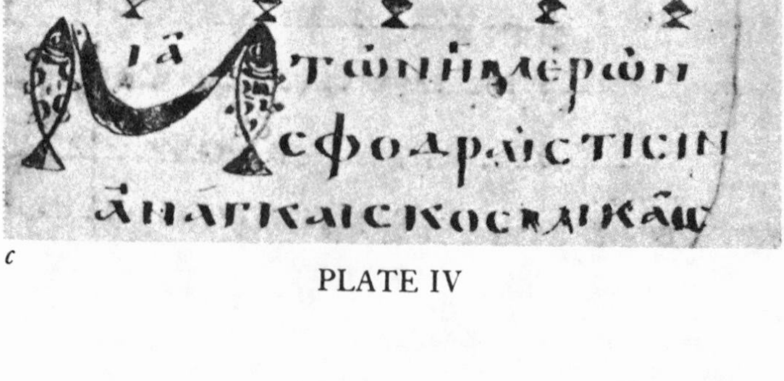

c

PLATE IV

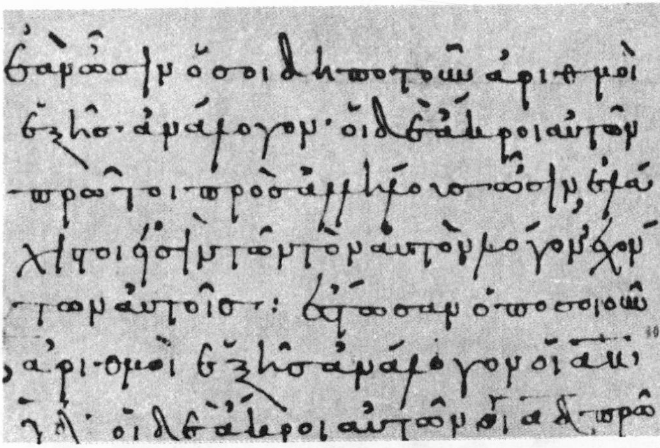

a

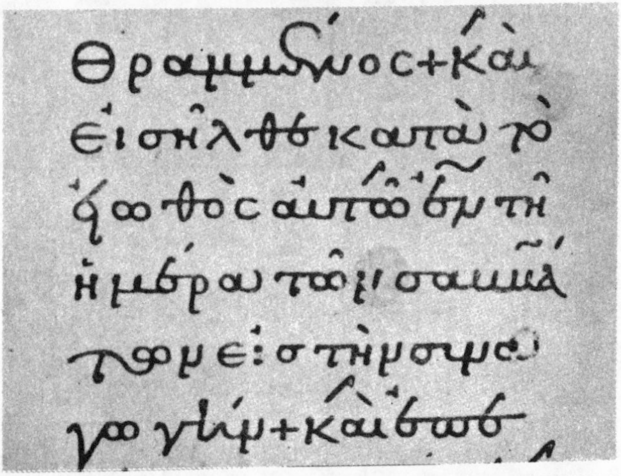

b

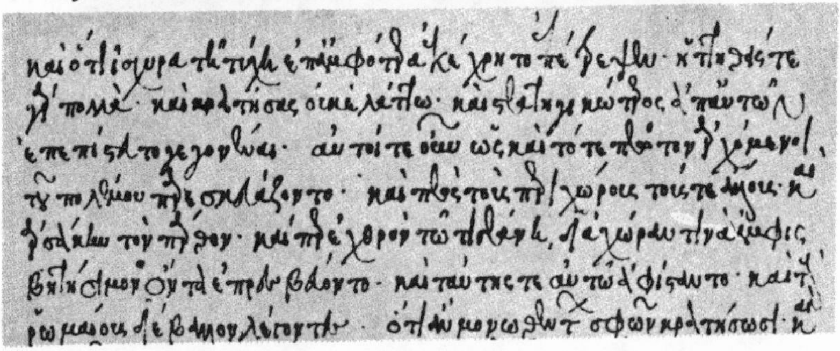

c

PLATE V

POSSVMVSHINCNE MESSISQ· DILATEMVS VSQ· SERENE

HQVANDOINHIDVMRENVSINPELLEREMARARA

CONVENTATQVANDONARMNASDEDVCEREL...

AVITEMELSTIVMISIVNSIVNVERTERIPINVM

a

QVIDSTRIISAVISCTLLAMIHE QVIDVASTACHARYSDIS

EAOIVITOPTATOCONDVNTVNTHYBRIDISALVEO·

SECVRIFELACIAIQ·MIHIMAAS STADIAECENIEM

INIMANINLAEIIHUMVALVITCONCESSITINIRAS

b

PLATE VI

c

a

NULLAMINSUOMACOMPUTABAM
SIOUUEREHOCTERTIOFUNCERETFACILI
OREONOHIEXCUSATIONEMFORESI
QUISINCIDISSETQUEMNONDEBEREM

b

PERCUPIOIPAEMUNO MULTAMIRA
FACIUNT SINISTRAOPERATURNON
DEXTERA DEXTRADEBETOPERARI
SIENESCIENIESINISTRA UTNECOMIS
CEATSECUPIOITASSAECUL QUANDO

c

PLATE VII

a

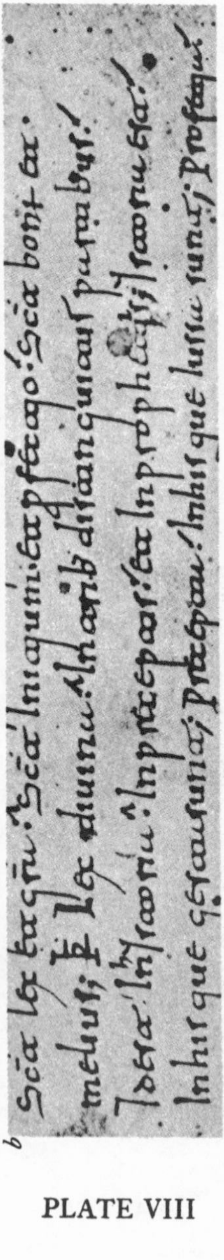
b

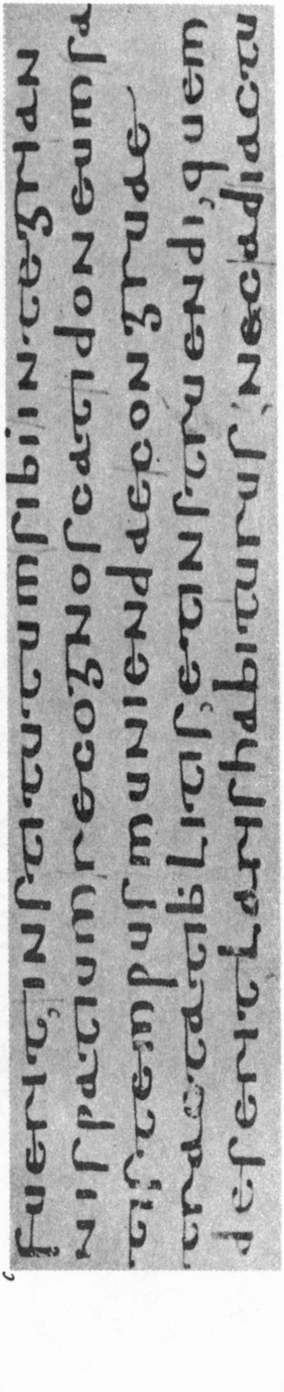
c

PLATE VIII

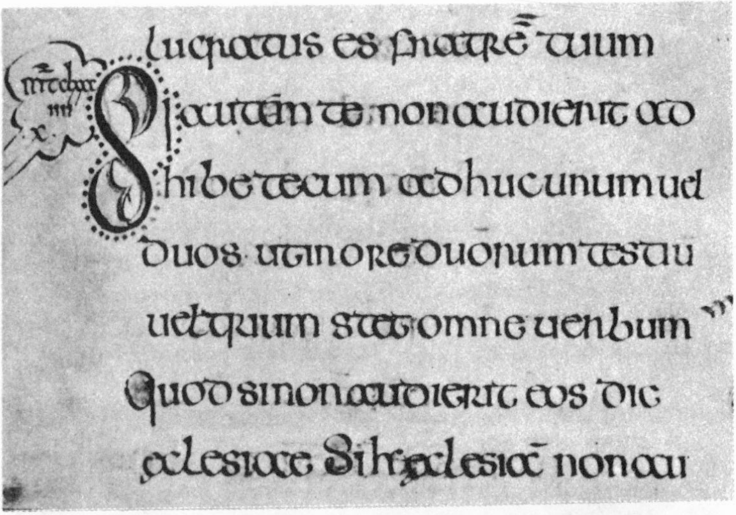

a

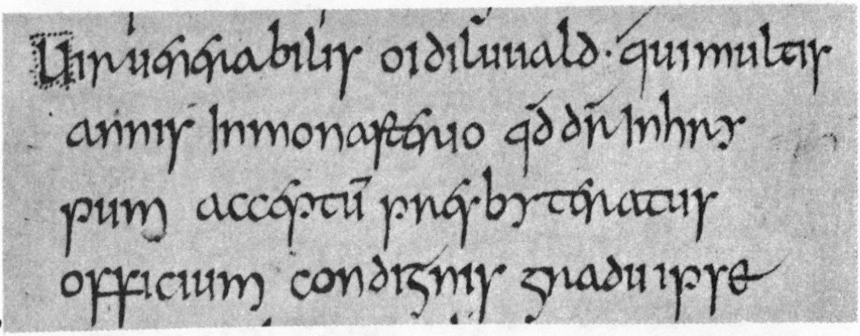

b

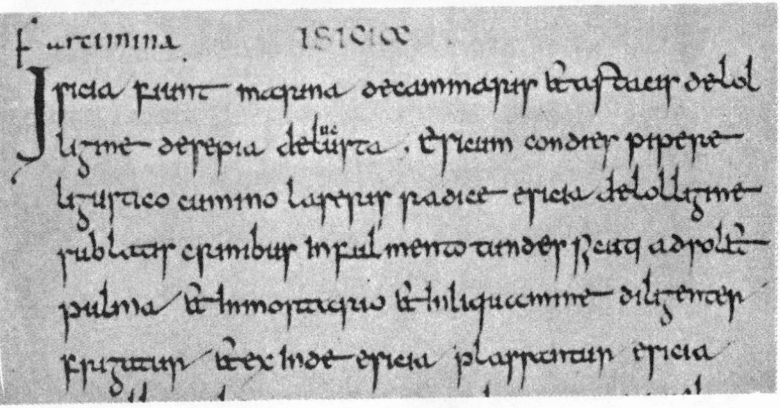

c

PLATE IX

a

quentibus disciplinis. I
de mathematica
Mathematica latine dicitur doctrinalis
scientia quae abstractam considerat
quantitatem. Abstractam enim
quantitatem quam intellectu a materia
vel abstrahentes a se credimus

b

sequebamur. In ath
et seminudus habet nis
rasibus per occultat o
sibi uestimentum dat. Tunc
ille accessit ad archidia
cono iussit algenat sine

c

acharesq; et tales bonas. neq; artes. neq; ehis
cui quas praeest. Incarptus ptarus cupidini
b; ad inteies ca et uoluptatess corpohs
pessumdat; e. pciosa hibidine p uls p
ul; ubi socordia uses. atmp; Ingenui diffluxe
te. noat Inspmacs accusatur. uatnqq;

PLATE X

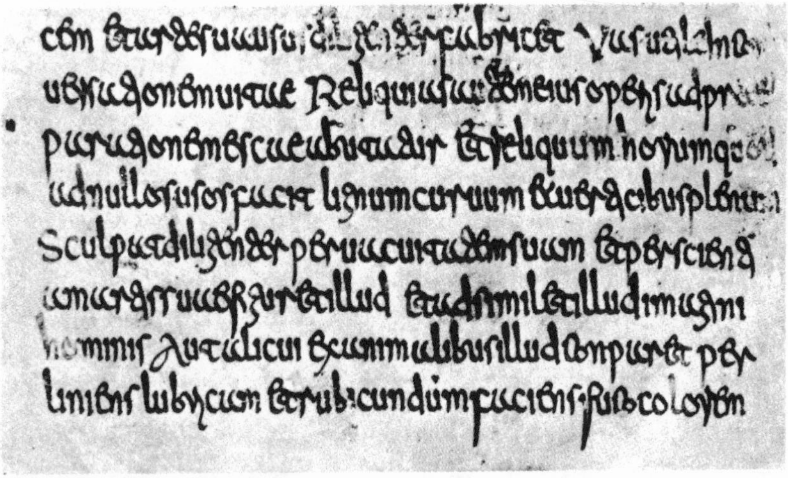

a

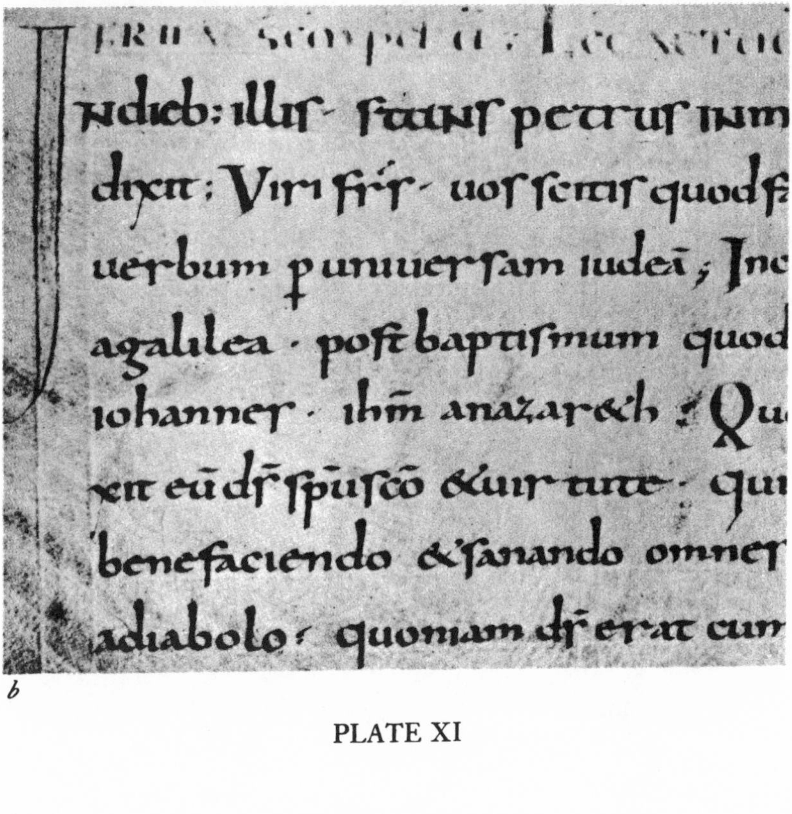

b

PLATE XI

a

co xxxem maiore adicies superioribus diebus fuerit uel decexcref:
indiraorum quae eadem diem firma steterat cum laborare coe
praenullae profecto diuidere quaecumquod spexuerant deimperio
defecere autem adpoenos hi publicae licent calcani hirpini

b

scrupulos iii · Cardamomi scrupulos vi · Cumini scor:
pulos vi · foliscrupulouno · Menta sicca scrupulos
vi · Tunsi cribrataq · melle colligis scōopus fuerit. li
quam ex excetii addis Alit piperis unc · i · petroselini
caret ligustici unc singulas melle colligunt ut cum

c

O CEANI PARS CELSA SUBHORRIFERO AQUILONE
A XEM OBITAE DEXTRA LEUAQUE TUENTUR
S IUE ARGTOAE SEU ROMANI COGNOMINIS URSAE
P LAUSTRA QUAEQ FACIES STELLARU PROXIMA UERO

PLATE XII

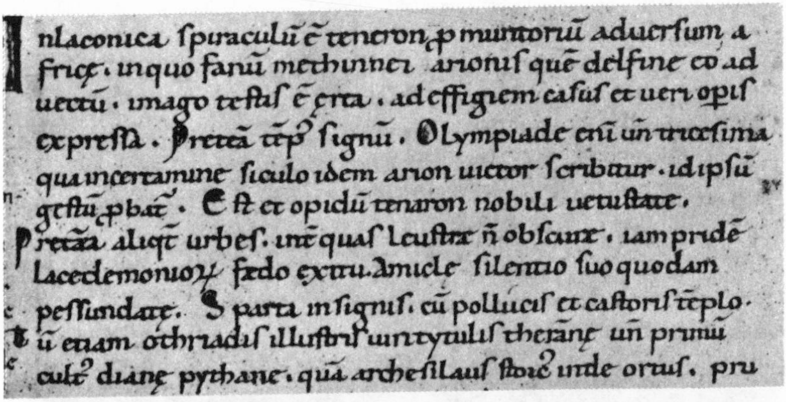

a

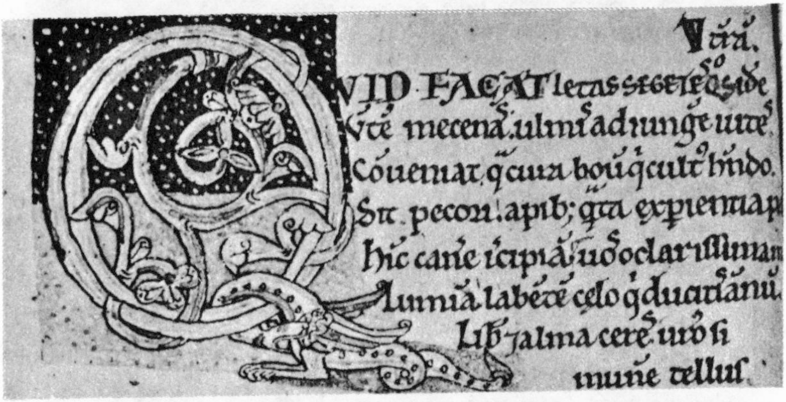

b

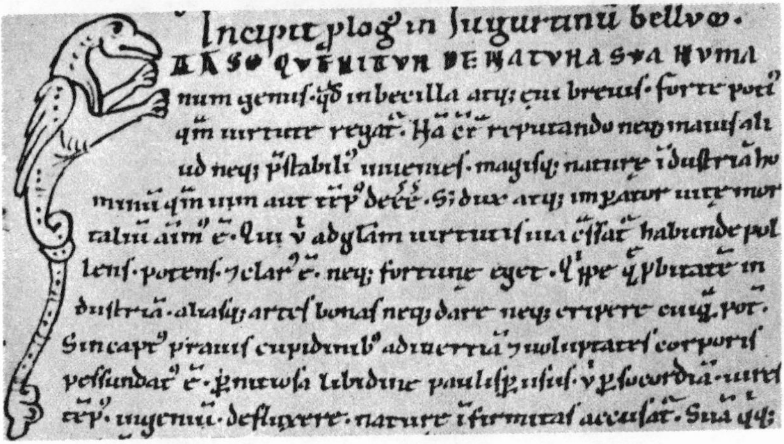

c

PLATE XIII

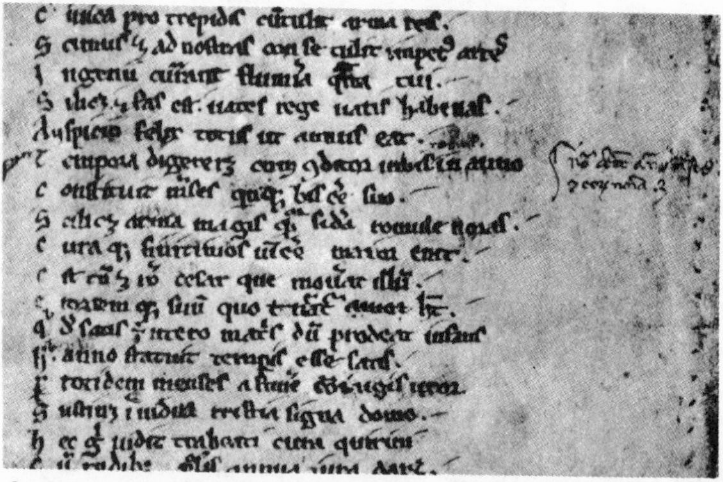

a

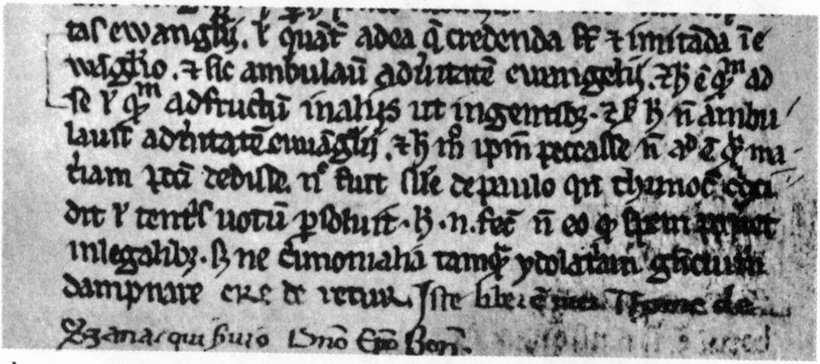

b

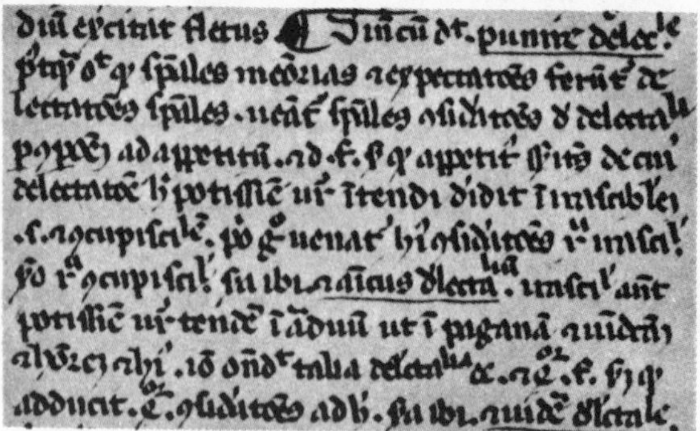

c

PLATE XIV

a

H unc q̄ nr̄as respice tr̄as .
E t siqua nouo bellua uultu
Q uatiet populos terrore graui
T u fulminibz frange trisulcis .
f oetus ip̄e genitore tuo
f ulmina mittes . al' mittens

Lucii Annei senece . hercules oetheus ex
plicit . feliciter . tragedia x̄ . Coluaus sye
nius manu propria scripsi .

b

ipsius qd ulla esse poterat lege lata . Sed cum mihi . p . c . &
pro me aliqd & in . M . antonium multa dicenda sint alterū
peto a uobis ut pro me dicentē benigne . alterum ipse efficiā
ut contra illum cum dicam attente audiatis . Simul illud
oro si meam cū in omni uita . tū in dicendo moderationem
modestiāq; cognoscatis ne me hodie cū isti ut prouocauit re
spondebo . oblitum esse putetis mei . Non tractabo ut consulē .
ne ille qd me ut consularem . & si ille nullo modo consul : uel

c

PLATE XV

Q uicquid agit: sanguis est tamen illa tuus.
S ed modo culta doce quamuis non uicta ligatos
I mpediat et in es nec stola longa pedes.
E t mihi sint dure leges laudare nec ullam
P ossum ego quin oculos appetat illa meos.
E t si quid peccasse putat ducoque capillis.
I mmerito proprias proripiorque uias.

pene ciuitatem exhausisse florentinos,
preter ciuiles discordias, peste q ferme ad i-
ternitionem consumptos: Roma morbo
continuo agitatam, uix unq fuisse inco
lumem. Quid febres referam, Quid capi-
tis, et totius corporis dolores: Quid flux'
uentris, et piculosissimas disenterias: r
Quid, quos ego paucis ante mensibus, ex-

Et sedeo duras iamtior ante fores.
No ego laudari curo mea delia tecu
Du mo sim quaeso segnis inersque nocer.
Et specte suprema mihi cu uenerit hora.
Et teneam moriens deficiente manu.
Flebis et arsuro positu me delia lecto.
Tristibus et lacrimis oscula mixta dabis.
Flebis no tua sunt duro pcordia ferro.

PLATE XVI

NOTES AND BIBLIOGRAPHY

NOTES

1. Thomas Astle, *The Origin and Progress of Writing*, London, 1784, 1803, p. i.

2. James H. Breasted, *The Conquest of Civilization*, New York, 1926, pp. 53–54.

3. It has even been suggested that the Semitic alphabet was known in Cappadocia in the third millennium B.C. (F. J. Stephens in *Journal of the American Oriental Society*, XLIX. 122–127, 1929). But the evidence is circumstantial and cannot be accepted until confirmed by other material. It has been claimed that the cuneiform alphabet found at Ras Shamra is independent of the Semitic alphabet, but Olmstead (see Bibliography under Sprengling) derives it from the Semitic.

4. Cf. *Cambridge Ancient History*, II, 1924, 487 ff. and the bibliography there given, especially John L. Myres and K. T. Frost, " The Historical Background of the Trojan War," in *Klio*, XIV. 447–467 (1915). The earlier attitude toward tradition is well shown by E. S. Roberts, *Introduction to Greek Epigraphy*, I, 1887, p. 2: " Tradition then must be treated as though it did not exist."

5. The name (" double gamma ") is a relatively late one derived from its resemblance to gamma.

6. Keil, *Grammatici Latini*, VII, 8–9.

7. The letter Z is found in an old prayer (vouched for by Varro and Velius Longus) called the *Carmen Saliare*.

8. Tacitus, *Ann.*, XI. 14.

9. The earliest dated inscription showing the use of a double consonant is of the year 189 B.C., while the earliest datable example of a double vowel belongs to the year 132 B.C.

10. Henry A. Sanders, *The New Testament Manuscripts in the Freer Collection* (University of Michigan Studies, Humanistic Series, Vol. IX), 1918, p. 139.

11. *The Classical Review*, VIII. 81 (1894).

12. A sample is given in a leaflet attached to numbers of the *Classical Review* for 1927. A new Greek type, based on ninth-century minuscule, has been designed by Francis H. Fobes under the name " Benner Greek " (Snail's Pace Press, Amherst, Mass., 1932).

13. Magnus Hammarström, *Om runskriftens härkomst* (Studier i Nordisk Filologi), Helsingfors, 1929.

14. Aem. Huebner, *Exempla Scripturae Epigraphicae Latinae*, Berlin, 1885, No. 1147.

15. *Ibid.*, No. 1148.

16. Paul Lehmann in L. Traube, *Vorlesungen und Abhandlungen*, I, 1909, pp. 171 ff.

17. B. L. Ullman in *Classical Philology*, XXIV. 294–297 (1929).

18. Further distinguishing marks of early Latin uncial are given by E. A. Lowe and E. K. Rand, *A Sixth-Century Fragment of the Letters of Pliny the Younger*, Washington, 1922, p. 19.

19. E. A. Lowe, " A Hand-List of Half-Uncial Manuscripts," in *Miscellanea Fr. Ehrle*, IV, Roma, 1924, p. 34 (vol. 40 of *Studi e Testi*).

20. Most recently Wilhelm Köhler, *Die Karolingischen Miniaturen, Erster Band: Die Schule von Tours*, Berlin, 1930.

21. Edward Kennard Rand, *A Survey of the Manuscripts of Tours*, Cambridge, 1929, and in *The Harvard Theological Review*, XXIV. 323–396 (1931).

22. Cesare Foligno, *Latin Thought during the Middle Ages*, Oxford, 1929, p. 61.

23. The parallelism between art and script is developed in a somewhat different way by Rudolf Kautsch, *Wandlungen in der Schrift und in der Kunst*, Mainz, 1929. In a rather theoretical fashion Kautsch contrasts the dynamic movement and expressionism of Merovingian, Gothic, and Baroque art and writing with the restful quiet and beauty of Carolingian, Renaissance, and classicistic.

24. Olga Dobiache Rojdestvensky, " Quelques considérations sur les origines de l'écriture dite ' gothique,' " in

Mélanges d'histoire du moyen âge offerts à M. Ferdinand Lot, Paris, 1925, pp. 691 ff. But see Luigi Schiaparelli, "Note paleografiche e diplomatiche," in *Archivio storico italiano*, LXXXVII. 12 (1929).

25. W. Meyer, "Die Buchstaben-Verbindungen der sogenannten gothischen Schrift," in *Abhandlungen der königlichen Gesellschaft der Wissenschaft zu Göttingen, Philologisch-Historische Klasse, Neue Folge*, I, 6, p. 97 (1897).

26. *Epist. fam.* XXIII. 19: *Non vaga quidem ac luxurianti littera, qualis est scriptorum seu verius pictorum nostri temporis longe oculos mulcens, prope autem afficiens ac fatigans, quasi ad aliud quam ad legendum sit inventa . . . sed alia quadam castigata et clara seque ultro oculis ingerente.*

27. F. Novati, *Epistolario di Coluccio Salutati*, Rome, 1896, III, p. 76: *Interim te rogatum velim quod epistolas Petri Abaialardi, si non habes, inquiri facias et ex tuis vel repertis studeas meo nomine quanto correctius poterit exemplari. Sed si de antiqua littera haberi possent, libentius acciperem; nullae quidem litterae sunt meis oculis gratiores.* The word *sed* seems to indicate that he prefers an old manuscript to one copied specially for him.

28. Facsimile in P. Schmiedeberg, *De Asconi codicibus et de Ciceronis scholiis Sangallensibus*, Breslau, 1905. Novati's statement (*Epistolario di Coluccio Salutati*, III, 1896, p. 656, note 1) that Florence, Laur. 48.22, an autograph of Poggio's, was written in 1403 is wrong; it dates from 1425 (E. Walser, *Poggius Florentinus*, Leipzig, 1914, p. 105, note 1; A. C. Clark, *The Vetus Cluniacensis of Poggio*, Oxford, 1905, p. lxii).

29. Thomas Francis Carter, *The Invention of Printing in China and Its Spread Westward*, New York, 1925, p. 101.

30. There are some fragments of books attributed to Gutenberg which seem to belong to an earlier date. This is particularly true of a calendar of 1448. Claims are made also for a "Sibyllenbuch" of 1444 or 1445 (B. A. Uhlendorf, "The Invention of Printing and Its Spread till 1470," in *The Library Quarterly*, II. 179–231, 1932). The claims for even earlier Dutch printing are still being pressed.

31. Recently claims have been made in favor of a *Passio Christi* as the first book printed in Italy (about 1462).

32. Daniel Berkeley Updike, *Printing Types*, Cambridge, 1922, I, p. 20.

33. An earlier Greek system represented some of the numerals by the initial letters of their names, *e.g.* H for *hekaton*, " hundred."

34. A sheet of papyrus roughly made by me in the ancient manner from strips cut on the Anapo River near Syracuse, Sicily, in 1926, still holds together in spite of the fact that no paste was used and that the sheet was merely pressed in a book.

35. F. Cumont, " Le plus ancien parchemin grec," in *Revue de Philologie*, XLVIII. 97 (1924) ; a reproduction in *New Palaeographical Society*, London, 1926, Series II, Plate 156.

36. Allen W. Seaby, *The Roman Alphabet and Its Derivatives*, London, 1925, p. 1.

BIBLIOGRAPHY

To supplement this brief sketch the reader is referred to the following selected list of books, many of which give more extended bibliographies. Books mentioned in the Notes are not repeated here. A superior number immediately following a book title indicates the edition.

ABBOTT, F. F., " The Evolution of the Modern Forms of the Letters of the Alphabet," in *Society and Politics in Ancient Rome*, pp. 234–259. New York, 1909. (For Chapter V.)

BUTIN, ROMAIN F., " The Serâbît Inscriptions," in *The Harvard Theological Review*, XXI. 9–67 (1928). (For Chapter II.)

—— " The Protosinaitic Inscriptions," in *The Harvard Theological Review*, XXV. 130–203 (1932). (For Chapter II.)

CAGNAT, R., *Cours d'Épigraphie Latine*,⁴ pp. 1–34. Paris, 1914. (For Chapters V and XVI.)

Cambridge Ancient History, IV, pp. 395–403 (by R. S. Conway). Cambridge, 1926. (For Chapter IV.)

CLARK, CHARLES UPSON, *Collectanea Hispanica* (Transactions of the Connecticut Academy of Arts and Sciences, 24). Paris, 1920. (For Chapter VIII.)

CROUS, ERNST, und KIRCHNER, JOACHIM, *Die gotische Schriftarten*. 64 Plates. Leipzig, 1928. (For Chapters X and XII.)

DEGERING, HERMANN, *Die Schrift*. 240 plates (sixth century B.C. to eighteenth A.D., Latin). Berlin, 1929.

DELITSCH, HERMANN, *Geschichte der abendländischen Schreibschriftformen*. Leipzig, 1928.

DIEHL, E., *Inscriptiones Latinae*. Bonn, 1912.

EGBERT, J. C., *Introduction to the Study of Latin Inscriptions*, pp. 17–71. New York, 1906. (For Chapters V and XVI.)

EHRLE, FRANCISCUS, et LIEBAERT, PAULUS, *Specimina Codicum Latinorum Vaticanorum*.² 50 plates. Berlin, 1927.

EVANS, ARTHUR J., " The European Diffusion of Pictography and Its Bearings on the Origin of Script," in R. R. Marett, *Anthropology and the Classics*, pp. 9–43. Oxford, 1908. (For Chapter I.)

[231]

—— *Scripta Minoa*, I. Oxford, 1909. (For Chapter I.)

FRANCHI DE' CAVALIERI, PIUS, et LIETZMANN, IOHANNES, *Specimina Codicum Graecorum Vaticanorum*.[2] 60 plates. Berlin, 1929.

GARDINER, A. H., "The Egyptian Origin of the Semitic Alphabet," in *The Journal of Egyptian Archaeology*, III. 1–16 (1916). (For Chapter II.)

GARDTHAUSEN, V., *Das alte Monogramm*. Leipzig, 1924. (For Chapter XV.)

—— *Griechische Palaeographie*.[2] 2 vols. Leipzig, 1911–1913.

GERCKE, ALFRED, und NORDEN, EDUARD, *Einleitung in die Altertumswissenschaft*,[3] I. Leipzig, 1927. (F. Hiller von Gaertringen, *Griechische Epigraphik;* Wilhelm Schubart, *Papyruskunde;* Paul Maas, *Griechische Paläographie;* H. Dessau, *Lateinische Epigraphik;* Paul Lehmann, *Lateinische Paläographie*.)

HAMMARSTRÖM, M., "Die antike Buchstabennamen," in *Arctos: Acta Historica Philologica Philosophica Fennica*, I. Fasc. 1–2, pp. 3–40 (1930). (For Chapter XIV.)

HERMANN, EDUARD, "Herkunft und Alter der deutschen Buchstabennamen," in *Nachrichten von der Gesellschaft der Wissenschaften zu Göttingen*, Phil.-Hist. Kl. 215–232 (1929). (For Chapter XIV.)

HILL, G. F., *The Development of Arabic Numerals in Europe*. Oxford, 1915. (For Chapter XVI.)

IHM, MAXIMILIAN, *Palaeographia Latina*. Leipzig, 1909.

JENSEN, HANS, *Geschichte der Schrift*. Hannover, 1925. (Brief description of many forms of writing, alphabetic and non-alphabetic. Well illustrated.)

JOHNSTON, H. W., *Latin Manuscripts*. Chicago, 1897.

KERN, O. *Inscriptiones Graecae*. Bonn, 1913.

KIRCHHOFF, A. *Studien zur Geschichte des griechischen Alphabets*. Gütersloh, 1887.

LARFELD, W., *Griechische Epigraphik*[3] (Handbuch der Altertumswissenschaft, I, 5), I, pp. 330–434. Munich, 1914. (For Chapter III.)

—— *Handbuch der griechischen Epigraphik*, I. Leipzig, 1907. (For Chapter III.)

BIBLIOGRAPHY

LEIBOVITCH, J., " Die Petrie'schen Sinai-Schriftdenkmäler," in *Zeitschrift der Deutschen Morgenländischen Gesellschaft*, LXXXIV. 1–14 (1930). Plates and bibliography. (For Chapter II.)

LINDBLOM, JOH., " Zur Frage der Entstehung des Alphabets," in *Bulletin de la Société Royale des Lettres de Lund 1931–1932, III* (1930). (For Chapter II.)

LINDSAY, WALLACE MARTIN, *Notae Latinae*. Cambridge, England, 1915. (For Chapter XV.)

LÖFFLER, K., *Einführung in die Handschriftenkunde*. Leipzig, 1929.

LOEW, E. A., *The Beneventan Script*. Oxford, 1914.

LOWE, E. A., " Handwriting," in C. G. Crump, *The Legacy of the Middle Ages*, pp. 197–226. Oxford, 1926.

MALLERY, GARRICK, *Pictographs of the North American Indians — Preliminary Paper* (Fourth Annual Report of the Bureau of Ethnology, 1882–1883). Washington, 1886. (For Chapter I.)

—— *Picture-Writing of the American Indians*. (Tenth Annual Report of the Bureau of Ethnology, 1888–'89). Washington, 1893. (For Chapter I.)

MASON, WILLIAM A., *A History of the Art of Writing*. New York, 1920.

MENTZ, ARTHUR, *Geschichte der griechisch-römischen Schrift*. Leipzig, 1920. (Full of interesting suggestions, not all of which are well grounded.)

New English Dictionary. Oxford. (For Chs. XII and XIV.)

OSWALD, JOHN CLYDE, *A History of Printing*. New York, 1928.

PEDDIE, R. A., *Printing: A Short History of the Art*. London, 1927.

ROBERTS, E. S., *Introduction to Greek Epigraphy*, I, pp. 1–22. Cambridge, England, 1887. (For Chapter III.)

SANDYS, SIR J. E., *Latin Epigraphy* [2] (Revised by S. G. Campbell), pp. 34–56. Cambridge, England, 1927. (For Chapters V and XVI.)

SCHIAPARELLI, LUIGI, *Avviamento allo studio delle abbreviature latine nel medioevo*. Florence, 1926.

—— *La Scrittura latina nell' età romana*. Como, 1921.

SCHUBART, WILHELM, *Griechische Palaeographie* (Handbuch der Altertumswissenschaft, I, 4, 1). Munich, 1925.

SCHULZE, W., " Die lateinischen Buchstabennamen," in *Sitzungsberichte der königl. preussischen Akademie der Wissenschaften*, 760–785 (1904). (For Chapter XIV.)

SMITH, DAVID EUGENE, and KARPINSKI, LOUIS CHARLES, *The Hindu-Arabic Numerals*. Boston, 1911. (For Chapter XVI.)

SPRENGLING, MARTIN, *The Alphabet: Its Rise and Development from the Sinai Inscriptions*. Chicago, 1931. (The latest complete interpretation of the Sinai inscriptions.) (For Chapter II.)

STEFFENS, FRANZ, *Lateinische Paläographie.*[2] Trier, 1909. (125 large plates with transcriptions. Introduction to palaeography.)

—— *Proben aus griechischen Handschriften.* 24 plates. Trier, 1912.

TAYLOR, ISAAC, *The History of the Alphabet.*[2] London, 1899. (Out of date in part.)

THOMPSON, SIR EDWARD MAUNDE, *An Introduction to Greek and Latin Palaeography*. 250 facsimiles. Oxford, 1912.

TRAUBE, LUDWIG, *Nomina Sacra*. Munich, 1907. (For Chapter XV.)

—— *Vorlesungen und Abhandlungen.* 3 vols. Munich, 1909–1920.

ULLMAN, B. L., " The Added Letters of the Greek Alphabet," in *Classical Philology*, XXII. 136–141 (1927). (For Chapter III.)

—— " The Etruscan Origin of the Roman Alphabet and the Names of the Letters," in *Classical Philology*, XXII. 372–377 (1927). (For Chapters IV and XIV.)

—— " The Origin and Development of the Alphabet," in *American Journal of Archaeology*, XXXI. 311–328 (1927). (For Chapter II.)

VAN HOESEN, HENRY BARTLETT, and WALTER, FRANK KELLER, *Bibliography: Practical, Enumerative, Historical*. New York, 1928. (Chapters on history of writing, printing, etc.)

SUPPLEMENTARY BIBLIOGRAPHY

BAINS, D., *A Supplement to Notae Latinae*. Cambridge, 1936.
BATTELLI, G., *Acta Pontificum* (Exempla Scripturarum, III²). Vatican City, 1965.
—— *Lezioni di Paleografia.*³ Vatican City, 1949.
BISCHOFF, B. *Mittelalterliche Studien.* 2 vols. Stuttgart, 1966–1967.
—— *Paläographie, mit besonderer Berücksichtigung des deutschen Kulturgebietes*, reprinted from *Deutsche Philologie im Aufriss.*² Berlin, Bielefeld, and Munich, 1957.
—— *Die südostdeutschen Schreibschulen und Bibliotheken in der Karolingerzeit; I, Die Bayrischen Diözesen.*² Wiesbaden, 1960.
BISCHOFF, B., AND HOFMANN, J., *Libri Sancti Kyliani, Die Würzburger Schreibschule und die Dombibliothek im VIII. und IX. Jahrhundert.* Wurzburg, 1952.
BISCHOFF, B., LIEFTINCK, G. I., AND BATTELLI, G., *Nomenclature des Écritures Livresques.* CNRS, Paris, 1954.
BROWN, T. J., "*Latin Palaeography Since Traube,*" *Transactions of the Cambridge Bibliographical Society*, III. 361–381 (1959–1963).
BRUCKNER, A., *Scriptoria Medii Aevi Helvetica*, I–XI. Geneva, 1935–1967——.
BRUCKNER, A., AND MARICHAL, R., *Chartae Latinae Antiquiores*, I–III. Olten and Lausanne, 1954–1967——.
BÜHLER, C. F., *The Fifteenth-Century Book: the Scribes, the Printers, the Decorators.* Philadelphia, 1960.
CASAMASSIMA, E., *Trattati di Scrittura del Cinquecento Italiano.* Milan, 1966.
CENCETTI, G., *Lineamenti di Storia della Scrittura Latina.* Bologna, 1954.
ČERNÝ, J., *Paper and Books in Ancient Egypt.* University College, London, 1952.

SUPPLEMENTARY BIBLIOGRAPHY

CHADWICK, J., *The Decipherment of Linear B*. Cambridge, 1958.

COHEN, M., *L'Écriture*. Paris, 1953.

DAIN, A., *Les Manuscrits*.² Paris, 1964.

DELAISSÉ, L. M. J., *Le Manuscrit autographe de Thomas à Kempis et 'l'Imitation de Jésus-Christ': Examen archéologique et édition diplomatique du Bruxellensis 3851–61*," Publications de Scriptorium, II. 2 vols. Brussels, 1956.

———— *La Miniature flamande: le Mécénat de Philippe le Bon* (Exhibition in Brussels and Paris). Brussels, 1959.

DESTREZ, J., *La Pecia dans les manuscrits universitaires du XIIIe et du XIVe siècle*. Paris, 1935.

DEVRÉESSE, R., *Introduction à l'Étude des manuscrits grecs*. Paris, 1954.

———— *Les manuscrits grecs de l'Italie méridionale* (Studi e Testi, 183). Vatican City, 1955.

DIRINGER, D., *Writing* (Ancient Peoples and Places Series). London, 1962.

DRIVER, G. R., *Semitic Writing*.² The British Academy, London, 1954.

———— *The Judaean Scrolls: the Problem and a Solution*. Oxford, 1965.

Early English Manuscripts in Facsimile, I–XV. Copenhagen, 1951–1968————.

L'Écriture et la psychologie des peuples. Centre International de Synthèse, Paris, 1963. (The chapters include: J. Février on Semitic writing, A. Dain on Greek writing, R. Bloch on Etruscan and Roman writing, R. Marichal on medieval writings, and H. J. Martin on printing.)

FAIRBANK, A. J., *A Book of Scripts*.⁵ Penguin Books, 1960.

FAIRBANK, A. J. AND HUNT, R. W., *Humanistic Script of the Fifteenth and Sixteenth Centuries* (Bodleian Library Picture Books, 12). Oxford, 1960.

FAIRBANK, A. J., AND WOLPE, B., *Renaissance Handwriting*. London, 1960.

FEBVRE, L., AND MARTIN, H. J., *L'Apparition du livre*. Paris, 1958.

[236]

SUPPLEMENTARY BIBLIOGRAPHY

FEDERICI, V., *La Scrittura delle Cancellerie Italiane dal Secolo XII al XVII*. 2 vols. Rome, 1934.

FOERSTER, H., *Abriss der lateinischen Paläographie.*[2] Stuttgart, 1963.

GRONINGEN, B. A. VAN, *Short Manual of Greek Palaeography*. Leyden, 1955.

HAJNAL, I., *L'Enseignement de l'écriture aux universités médiévales*. Budapest, 1959.

HIGOUNET, C., *L'Écriture* (Collection "Que sais-je?"). Paris, 1955.

IRIGOIN, J., "Pour une Étude des centres de copie Byzantins," in *Scriptorium,* XII. 208–227 (1958).

JEFFERY, L. M., *The Local Scripts of Archaic Greece.* Oxford, 1961.

JOHNSON, A. F., *Type Designs: their Development and History.*[3] London, 1966.

KENYON, F. G., *Books and Readers in Ancient Greece and Rome.*[2] Oxford, 1951.

KER, N. R., *Catalogue of Manuscripts containing Anglo-Saxon.* Oxford, 1957.

——— *English Manuscripts in the Century after the Norman Conquest.* Oxford, 1960.

KIRCHNER, J., *Scriptura Gothica Libraria.* Munich and Vienna, 1966.

KLAFFENBACH, G., *Griechische Epigraphik.* Göttingen, 1957.

KRUITWAGEN, B., *Laat-Middeleeuwsche Paleografica, Paleotypica . . . .* The Hague, 1942.

LAKE, K., AND LAKÊ, S., *Dated Greek Minuscule Manuscripts to the Year 1200 A.D.* 11 vols. Boston, Massachusetts, 1934–1945.

LEHMANN, P. J. G., *Erforschung des Mittelalters.* 5 vols. Leipzig, later Stuttgart, 1941–1962.

LESNE, E., *Les Livres, 'Scriptoria' et Bibliothèques du commencement du VIIIe à la fin du XIe siècle* (Mémoires . . . par des professeurs des Facultés Catholiques de Lille, XLVI). 1938.

LIEFTINCK, G. I., *Manuscrits datés conservés dans les Pays-Bas: Catalogue paléographique . . . ,* I (2 parts). Amsterdam, 1964———.

SUPPLEMENTARY BIBLIOGRAPHY

Lowe, E. A., *Codices Latini Antiquiores,* I–XI. Oxford, 1934–1966——.
—— *English Uncial.* Oxford, 1960.
—— "A Key to Bede's Scriptorium: Some Observations on the Leningrad Manuscript of the 'Historia Gentis Anglorum'," in *Scriptorium,* XII. 182–190 (1958).
Mallon, J., *Paléographie Romaine.* Madrid, 1952.
Mallon, J., Marichal, R., and Perrat, C., *L'Écriture latine de la capitale romaine à la minuscule.* Paris, 1939.
Marinis, T. de, *La Biblioteca Napoletana dei Re d'Aragona.* 4 vols. Milan, 1952–1957.
Masai, F., "Paléographie et codicologie," in *Scriptorium,* IV. 279–293 (1950).
—— "La paléographie gréco-latine," in *Scriptorium,* X. 281–302 (1956).
Mentz, A., *Die Tironischen Noten.* Berlin, 1944.
Millares Carlo, A., *Tratado de Paleografía Española.* 2 vols. Madrid, 1932.
Milne, H. J. M., and Skeat, T. C., *Scribes and Correctors of the Codex Sinaiticus.* The British Museum, London, 1938.
Morison, Stanley, *American Copybooks.* Philadelphia, 1951.
—— *On Type Designs Past and Present, a Brief Introduction.*[2] London, 1962.
Mynors, R. A. B., *Durham Cathedral Manuscripts to the End of the Twelfth Century.* Durham, 1939.
Norsa, M., *La Scrittura Letteraria Greca.* Florence, 1939.
Ogg, O., *Three Classics of Italian Calligraphy . . . the Writing Books of Arrighi, Tagliente and Palatino.* Dover Books, 1953.
Osley, A. S. (ed.), *Calligraphy and Palaeography: Essays Presented to Alfred Fairbank.* London, 1965.
Perrat, C., Bischoff, B., and Post, G., papers on recent developments in Latin palaeography, in *Relazioni del X Congresso Internazionale di Scienze Storiche,* I. 345–422. Rome, 1955.
Petrucci, A., "Per la storia della scrittura romana. I graffiti di Condatamagos," in *Bulletino dell'Archivio Paleografico Italiano,* 3rd series, I, 85–132 (1962).

SUPPLEMENTARY BIBLIOGRAPHY

—— *La Scrittura di Francesco Petrarca* (Studi e Testi, 248). Vatican City, 1967.

REYNOLDS, L. D. AND WILSON, N. G., *Scribes and Scholars*, Oxford, 1968.

ROBERTS, C. H., "The Codex," in *Proceedings of the British Academy*, XL. 169–204 (1954).

—— *Greek Literary Hands, 350 B.C.–A.D. 400* (Oxford Palaeographical Handbooks Series). Oxford, 1956.

SAMARAN, C., AND MARICHAL, R., *Catalogue des Manuscrits en écriture latine portant des indications de date, de lieu ou de copiste*, I–III, V. Paris, 1959–1962, 1965——.

SCHOLDERER, V., *Johann Gutenberg*. The British Museum, London, 1963.

SCHUBART, W., *Das Buch bei den Griechen und Römern*.[3] Heidelberg, 1962.

SEIDER, R. *Paläographie der Griechischen Papyri*, I. Stuttgart, 1967——. (Plates of documents.)

SKEAT, T. C., "The Use of Dictation in Ancient Book-Production," in *Proceedings of the British Academy*, XLII. 179–208 (1956).

STEINBERG, S. H., *Five Hundred Years of Printing*.[3] Penguin Books, 1961.

STEVENSON, A., *Observations on Paper as Evidence*. University of Kansas Libraries, Lawrence, Kansas, 1961.

—— *The Problem of the Missale speciale*. The Bibliographical Society, London, 1967.

TJÄDER, J. O., *Die nichtliterarischen Papyri Italiens aus der Zeit 455–700* (Skrifter utgivna av Svenska Institutet i Rom, 4°, XIX. 2 vols.). Lund, 1954——.

TURNER, E. G., *Athenian Books in the fifth and fourth centuries B.C.* University College, London, 1952.

—— *Greek Papyri*. Oxford, 1968.

ULLMAN, B. L., *The Origin and Development of Humanistic Script*. Rome, 1960.

—— *The Humanism of Coluccio Salutati*. Padua, 1963.

Umbrae Codicum Occidentalium, I–XI. Amsterdam, 1960–1966——.

VAUX, R. DE, *L'Archéologie et les manuscrits de la Mer Morte*. The British Academy, London, 1961.

[239]

SUPPLEMENTARY BIBLIOGRAPHY

VENTRIS, M., AND CHADWICK, J., *Documents in Mycenaean Greek*. Cambridge, 1956.

WARDROP, J., *The Script of Humanism*. Oxford, 1963.

WITTEK, M., *Album de Paléographie grecque*. Ghent, 1967.

WOODHEAD, A. G., *The Study of Greek Inscriptions*. Cambridge, 1959.

YADIN, Y., *The Message of the Scrolls*. London, 1957.

To supplement this brief sketch the reader is referred to the following selected list of books, many of which give more extended bibliographies. Books mentioned in the Notes are not repeated here.

MEDIEVAL ACADEMY REPRINTS FOR TEACHING